CHRISTMAS IN CONNECTICUT

DIANE SMITH

GUILFORD, CONNECTICUT

Cover and text design by Nancy Freeborn

Library of Congress Cataloging-in-Publication Data
Smith, Diane.
    Christmas in Connecticut / Diane Smith.— 1st ed.
      p. cm.
    ISBN 0-7627-1018-7
    1. Christmas—Connecticut—History. 2. Connecticut—Social life and customs. I. Title.

GT4986.C8 S65 2001
394.2663'09746—dc21   2001045207

Manufactured in Canada
First Edition/First Printing

Contents

Feeling Festive

The Governor's Residence, Hartford

Christmas is on my mind all year. I'm always on the lookout for unusual ornaments for my tree—mementos of special occasions and of travels both near and far. As we decorate the tree, I love reminiscing with my husband, Tom, about the event that inspired the purchase of each one. These conversations breathe life into the memories and link the holiday season from year to year with the treasured moments in our lives.

The white-satin-and-lace–covered ball, embellished with opalescent seed pearls, is the most cherished ornament in my collection. It reminds me of a bridal gown, and Tom found it in a shop in New Haven the year we were married. There are tiny picture frames, each one holding a baby photo of our nephews. There are ornaments that look like our dogs, and one that looks like the cat we had years ago. Scatty is gone now, but her plump Persian likeness hangs on the tree each Christmas. The trio of Eiffel Towers was sent by my sister Melissa the year she moved to Paris. Unwrapping the replica of a humpback whale, I am transported for a moment to Maui. There's the blue crab from the Chesapeake, and a lobster claw hand-painted with a majestic tall ship. We found that one on the Cape, where we'd gone for a friend's wedding. We found the globes painted with images of Connecticut lighthouses at Mystic Seaport and the Maritime Aquarium in Norwalk. They hang alongside a miniature lobster trap from a long weekend with good friends in Maine. Christmas is about memories, family, and tradition. Decorating the tree each year is the touchstone that brings all of it together.

Sometime in late fall, when the last few leaves are clinging to the tree limbs, just before a cold blast of winter brushes them to the ground, the Christmas season actually kicks off. The phone rings. It's a friend at Easter Seals, asking me to record the narrative for the United Illuminating Fantasy of Lights, the holiday light show that opens in mid-November. Soon a team of volunteers will be busy in New Haven's Lighthouse Point Park, erecting the displays that will delight thousands of visitors throughout the season and raise funds to help people with disabilities all year long. The caring people who make the event a success, combined with the rainbow sparkle of lights that illuminate the dark winter nights, infuse the season with a spirit that you can almost touch. I start feeling festive from the moment we record the first few words that will welcome visitors to the park. That feeling lingers for weeks, renewed each time I step inside my home and flick on the lights on my own Christmas tree.

Connecticut's First Christmas Tree

Legend has it that the first Christmas tree in Connecticut (perhaps the first in New England) was decorated in 1777 by Hendrick Roddmore in Windsor Locks. He must have had many trees to choose from, for Windsor Locks at the time was known as Pine Meadow.

The Christmas tree is believed to have originated in Germany, Hendrick Roddmore's homeland. Roddmore was a Hessian soldier hired by the British to fight in the Revolutionary War. He was captured in 1776 in Bennington, Vermont, following Burgoyne's unsuccessful expedition into Vermont for supplies. Soon after his release, Roddmore was hired by Samuel Denslow to work on his farm in Pine Meadow. Denslow thought so highly of Roddmore that he built him a cabin on the farm, where Roddmore lived for fourteen years. To bring a touch of his native Germany to his new home, Roddmore is said to have decorated a Christmas tree in his cabin.

The legend has never been proved or disproved. Some are convinced that Roddmore's tree really was the first Christmas tree in the New World; there are accounts, however, of Christmas trees in Pennsylvania German communities as early as 1747. Connecticut did make history in 1845 when it became the fourth state in the Union and the first in New England to declare Christmas a legal holiday.

Alas, Christmas was not always a happy time for Hendrick Roddmore—his wife, Polly, died on December 25, 1790, at the age of forty. After her death, Roddmore moved from the Denslow farm to Windsor, where he became a shepherd and eventually remarried.

The Denslow farm is now known as Noden-Reed Park and is owned by the town of Windsor Locks and operated by the Windsor Locks Historical Society. The farm dates to 1762; the house and barn on the property were built in the mid-1800s. The barn is one of the few brick barns still standing in New England, and inside it visitors can view farm tools once used to cultivate tobacco, as well as a hand-painted medicine wagon. Inside the house at Christmastime, the Noden-Reed Park Museum holds Victorian Christmas Open House Days, giving visitors a taste of the holidays of yesteryear and paying tribute to Hendrick Roddmore's pioneering Christmas tree.

A Victorian Tree Extravaganza

Connecticut is rich with opportunities to celebrate the many traditions of Christmas, and no holiday would be complete without a visit to at least one of the many historic houses and museums in the state that deck the halls with style.

An extravaganza of Victorian trees is held each year at the Lockwood-Mathews Mansion Museum in Norwalk, and it's a delightful way to learn about the customs in decorating Christmas trees in the days when having one was a novelty.

LeGrand Lockwood would have enjoyed the holiday display of cast-iron toy trains in his former home. A railroad baron, Lockwood was able to see his own trains, the full-sized kind, from the windows of his sixty-two-room home. But it's unlikely the toy trains were ever set out under a Christmas tree there, because the house was the Lockwood and Mathews families' summer cottage in the tradition of the summer "cottages" of Newport (although it predated the Newport mansions by about twenty years).

LeGrand Lockwood was a Norwalk native and its first millionaire. The summer home he built in his hometown was one of the most splendid of his time. Today the mansion is a National Historic Landmark that's been featured on the A&E program *America's Castles*.

Although the families that owned the estate may never have spent Christmas here, it's fun to imagine how they might have celebrated the holidays. The museum's annual Victorian holiday exhibition gives a pretty good idea. In each of the downstairs rooms, a tree represents one of the Victorian decades from 1850 through 1910.

"Christmas trees were introduced into America in the latter part of the eighteenth century by German immigrants," says museum curator Susan Gunn. "But they did not become popular until *Godey's Lady's Book* published a picture of Queen Victoria and Prince Albert's tree in 1846. The tree in the Lockwood-Mathews Mansion's entrance hall is based on this photo." The small, tabletop tree is decorated with nuts, dried fruits, cookies, and sugarplums.

A few years later, Christmas trees featured candles wired to the branches. A small gift might be tied to a branch. Christmas trees were highly flammable, so the candles were lighted for only a few minutes, and a bucket of water was kept nearby to douse any flare-ups. "The tree was often placed near a window or door, so if it should catch fire, it could be tossed out of the house," Susan notes.

The music room's tree is typical of the 1870s, decorated with dried flowers, gilded nuts, and strings of popcorn and cranberries. Homemade decorations appeared on trees of this decade, and candles were attached with tin clips instead of wires. Small toys and gifts were tied onto the tree and removed on Christmas morning. "Of course, that left a bare-looking tree, so eventually gifts would be placed beneath the tree," says Susan. "More toys began to appear after the Civil War, as machine shops set up sidelines to produce them."

A new style of ornamentation developed when families cut out paper designs, known as scraps, from magazines to hang on their trees. Sometimes the scraps were pasted onto cookies and hung from narrow ribbons.

From the 1870s through the turn of the twentieth century, ornaments became more elaborate. Printmaking and papermaking processes advanced, and fancy paper cutouts were sold to be trimmed with tinsel and turned into tree decorations. Manufactured ornaments of glass, tin, and fabric appeared on trees. Blown eggs and popcorn garlands

remained popular, but they would soon be replaced by tinsel resembling icicles and by embossed paper with shimmery finishes that looked like pressed metal. While most gifts were placed beneath the tree, the custom continued of placing on the tree a gift envelope that might include a concert ticket or a letter from a sweetheart.

In the 1880s the earliest artificial trees were introduced to the United States from Germany. Goose feathers dyed green were attached to branches to resemble German white pines. The widely spaced branches accommodated newly popular glass ornaments.

The tree in the grand dining room at the Lockwood-Mathews Mansion is the most modern, representing the early 1900s. It's a tall tree, almost reaching the ceiling, and is illuminated with the electric lights introduced by

President Grover Cleveland in 1895.

On view in the dining room is a costume that might have been worn by a girl of the time. A Weston woman created it from a pattern published in a Victorian lady's magazine. The festive outfit features a cape of green cambric with tissue paper fringe. Popcorn garlands and shiny paper horns filled with sweets hang from the cape. A hoop attached to the hem creates the conelike shape of the evergreen tree. Bells sewn to the hem add to the holiday merriment, and the child would don a peaked felt cap to provide a proper top to the tree. It was the Victorian's ultimate holiday adornment, a living, breathing Christmas tree!

The nation's oldest public art museum—the Wadsworth Atheneum in Hartford—serves as a breathtaking backdrop for the annual Festival of Trees and Traditions. The two-story-high vaulted ceiling and crimson walls lined with art masterpieces in Morgan Great Hall is one of the settings for lavishly adorned trees, centerpieces, garlands, and holiday decorations, all available for sale. From late morning until late afternoon there is live entertainment on the hour, including musical performances by civic and school groups ranging from a Klezmer band to a string orchestra. Storytelling and crafts workshops for kids are offered in Candy Lane.

The weeklong festival celebrates Christmas, Hanukkah, Kwanzaa, Three Kings Day, and the winter solstice. Individual children and school groups are invited to participate in activities such as painting a *kinara* for Kwanzaa, playing dreidel games for Hanukkah, or adding their Christmas wishes to the children's tree. A boutique sells ornaments, candles, books, and small souvenirs for the kids. Organized by the Women's Committee of the Wadsworth Atheneum, it's the largest public fund-raiser for the museum and involves nearly three hundred volunteers. The proceeds help underwrite everything from children's art supplies and the conservation of paintings to a documentary film series, lectures, and other special events at the internationally recognized museum.

Christmas Impressions

On Christmas Day 1850, Florence Griswold was born into the illustrious Griswold family. The daughter of a wealthy sea captain, Miss Florence, as she came to be known, grew up in one of the largest and finest homes in the village of Old Lyme. Forty-nine years later, she opened her stately Georgian mansion as a boardinghouse for American impressionist artists, and they turned the architectural gem into an artistic masterpiece.

The painters Miss Florence called her "boys" changed the way Americans looked at the world. Her fields, farm, and the Lieutenant River that curved through her property inspired the artists.

"They very much loved the landscape and the sense of place that this corner of Connecticut and New England has, with all of its low-lying river areas," says Jeffrey Andersen, director of the Florence Griswold Museum, now a National Historic Landmark in Old Lyme's historic district.

The impressionist artists had great affection for the woman who opened not only her home but also her heart. Their gift and tribute to her were the works of art they left behind on her walls, mantelpieces, and wooden doors.

"One of the unusual features of the house itself are these painted door panels, which you see throughout the building." Jeffrey points out a door painted front and back by some of the greatest names in American art—Childe Hassam, Willard Metcalf, and William Chadwick.

Christmas here is extra special since it is also Miss Florence's birthday. Every year trees and holiday decorations inspired by the museum's art collection transform the house. A painting of Miss Florence's gardens motivates volunteers, who pluck blossoms of Queen Anne's lace in

summer, then dry the flowers and encrust the branches of evergreens with them.

Salmon- and cream-colored miniature poinsettias completely cover another tree. "We take the plants out of the pot and put them in little plastic bags, making sure the soil is very moist," explains Nancy Seymour, a volunteer decorator. "Then we tie up the top of the bag and put it into dark green florist's foil. We wrap twist-ties around the foil and twist-tie each one onto the tree."

A recent holiday celebration featured a series of historic vignettes re-creating the bohemian spirit of the Old Lyme art colony. In the parlor a mannequin portrayed Miss Florence celebrating her birthday by receiving guests. The dining room, famous for its many panels painted by the artists, was set for a holiday feast. Upstairs, three modern-day artists created festive displays using objects in the museum's collection. Don Male, an artist from Chester, made a mobile tree inspired by a collection of winter paintings. Connie Beale, an interior designer, turned her gallery into a winter wonderland with trees that seemed to emerge from the paintings hanging on the walls. Lyme designer Jean Callan King dipped into the museum's ceramics collection for her theme. And children from southeastern Connecticut created a birthday tree for Miss Florence.

Curator Jack Becker was delighted. "The artists met the challenge of creating surprising twists on holiday themes using unusual decorations and objects from our collections."

The Florence Griswold Museum is worth a visit any time of year, but especially at Christmas, when the house is lovingly decorated and the spirit of Florence Griswold abounds.

The Fairfield Christmas Tree Festival

Remember the way you felt as a child whenever you first glimpsed your Christmas tree? It seemed a magical thing, all glitter and sparkle, garland and twinkle. You'll feel that way again when you see the magic made by the decorators at the annual Fairfield Christmas Tree Festival, a three-day fund-raising event opening the first Thursday evening after Thanksgiving.

An army of volunteers transforms the Burr Homestead, a stately Greek revival home, into a glitzy winter showplace. Dozens of lavishly decorated trees fill each of the thirteen rooms, with mantelpieces and doorway swags to mix and match. One marble mantel might be mounded with sugar-frosted fruits and pheasant feathers; another room is outfitted baseboard to ceiling in the theme of storybook character Harry Potter. Every item is for sale, and volunteers will make custom wreaths for your door.

The festival started twenty years ago as a fund-raiser for the Barnum Festival, which celebrates the life of circus entrepreneur Phineas T. Barnum. Since then it has raised well over a million dollars for other nonprofits, including the American Cancer Society and the Center for Women and Families, which provides a haven for victims of domestic violence.

The Burr Homestead is one of the most historic homes in Fairfield County. Peter Burr built the original house on the site in 1700. It later belonged to his son Thaddeus. John Hancock and Dorothy Quincy were married there in 1775. Many of our young nation's greatest citizens are reported to have visited there, including George Washington, Benjamin Franklin, and John Adams. Aaron Burr, a cousin, was said to have been a frequent guest.

The Fairfield Christmas Tree Festival is kicked off by a gala preview party on the first Thursday evening after Thanksgiving. On Friday evening there's a special event for kids and their parents, followed by a walk to the town green for the arrival of Santa. Photos with Santa are taken throughout the weekend, and a gift boutique will help get you started on your shopping.

A Capitol Idea

Lofty inspirations often come from lofty locations. In the case of lighting up Hartford's Bushnell Park for the holidays, WTIC NewsTalk 1080's Ray Dunaway was gazing out the window of his studio on the nineteenth floor of the Gold Building one winter six years ago and saw a large patch of darkness in a city otherwise filled with light.

"There's nothing darker than New England on a December afternoon," says Ray, a native of the Midwest. "Here is this nice downtown and it's well lighted, and I look over at Bushnell Park and there's a black hole. I mean there's *nothing* there."

A lightbulb went off in his head: *Let's illuminate Bushnell Park for the holidays.*

"He had the idea, the vision, and the passion," says Lieutenant Governor Jodi Rell. "All he needed was a co-conspirator. That's when he called me."

The first year they lit one forty-foot tree, donated by a Berlin family after a storm uprooted it. The tree was flown in by helicopter and erected at the base of the Capitol. Six years later, sixty trees in America's oldest public park twinkle with more than half a million lights.

"You know how it is," says Ray. "Once you get started you don't want to stop." And as the display has gotten bigger and brighter, corporate donations have grown to pick up most of the tab.

The lieutenant governor and Ray host the Holiday in the Park Tree Lighting Ceremony in early December, featuring choirs and special appearances by the mayor, the governor, and Santa. It's a day everyone at the Capitol looks forward to, especially the lieutenant governor: "The park now stands as a beacon of holiday festivity and is, I think, the crown jewel of Hartford's holiday celebration."

Ray Dunaway, Diane Smith, and Lieutenant Governor Jodi Rell at the Bushnell Park tree lighting.

More Capital Lights

The Hartford Festival of Light sets Constitution Plaza aglow with two-hundred-thousand white lights from the day after Thanksgiving until Three Kings Day in January. Many people consider the lighting ceremony the official kickoff for the holiday season in the capital city. Santa Claus is the guest of honor at the lighting event, which is open to the public and features live music and a carol sing-along. The entire plaza is illuminated, along with a giant tree, a cascading waterfall in the fountain, and statues of angels and deer designed by the same artist whose sculptures adorn Rockefeller Center in New York City.

Christmas in the capital, clockwise from top left: Soldiers and Sailors Monument; lights wrap a tree; the Hartford Festival of Light on Constitution Plaza; the Hartford Stage Company.

Holiday Glow

The Bible says, "Let there be light," and in Connecticut there's plenty of it at Christmastime. Drive-through light shows are cropping up all over the state.

As you drive into *Hubbard Park* in Meriden, you pass beneath a sky full of snowflakes, sparkling with white lights. Emerging from a quiet wooded cove is a family of deer and, a little farther along, a mama bear and her cubs. Walter Hubbard, the industrialist who donated the land for Hubbard Park in the 1890s, would have loved this. His company, Bradley and Hubbard, produced gas and electric light fixtures. He also founded Meriden Electric Light. The park named after him is the largest municipal park in New England. It was designed by Frederick Law Olmsted, who designed New York's Central Park.

Meriden's Parks and Recreation Department employees create the display, with an emphasis on local culture. There's a lighted replica of Castle Craig, a Meriden landmark, and a field of daffodils, a reminder of the Daffodil Festival that is a highlight of spring. The beauty of the park adds to the show, with rows of trees beautifully electrified by white lights. Besides the dolphins leaping from the lake, there are horses trotting over snow-covered fields, turtles, elephants, camels, and moose. Lighted birds are perched in branches overhead. Ten trees are lit on the amphitheater stage, a bridge in the park is illuminated, and even the tennis courts and concession buildings are decked out in lights. In all there are four hundred thousand lights spread out over sixty-seven acres.

Hubbard Park is the only free light show in the state, and the only one you can also enjoy on foot. The show starts late in November with an evening of special activities including ice carving, music, and wagon rides. The lights stay on through the first week in January.

Passing through Morris Cove on the road to Lighthouse Point Park in New Haven will get you in the spirit for the *United Illuminating Fantasy of Lights*. Many of the homes along the route are decked out for the holidays, and you'll glimpse the light displays in the park reflected in the harbor as you round the bend of the cove.

Hubbard Park's holiday display includes swans on the lake and a replica of Castle Craig.

UI Fantasy of Lights helps light a flame of hope for people with disabilities in the greater New Haven area. The show is the biggest single fund-raiser of the year for Easter Seals Goodwill Industries, which changes lives every day by helping people with disabilities live independently and train for and hold good jobs.

The lighthouse that gives the park its name is outlined in lights, and you'll pass the park's historic restored carousel. Fantasy of Lights is organized into themed sections. Turn on your radio for holiday music, and a narrator (me!) guides you through Toyland, Candyland, the North Pole, and Winter Wonderland. Since the show is located at the most popular beach in New Haven, it naturally capitalizes on Summer Fun, featuring a sailboat, a tugboat, Santa on a Jet Ski, and a giant red lobster. Local companies sponsor the fifty displays, and they get bigger and more elaborate each year as sponsors add new features. Most spectacular are the deer leaping across the roadway, the ice tunnel, and the ringing bell and wreath arches that you pass under. Each scene is animated.

This is truly a community effort. The city donates the park space; local unions donate countless hours of labor to erect and light the displays. Each night a local company, organization, or family provides the volunteers (more than six hundred in all) to sell tickets and hand out programs. *Yankee* magazine named Fantasy of Lights a "must see" event. The show opens in mid-November and runs through New Year's Eve. All proceeds go to Easter Seals Goodwill Industries.

The newest of the light shows is *Park City Lights* in Bridgeport, which opened for the first time in 2000. The display is set up in Beardsley Park, and you'll catch sight of it from the I–95/Route 8 connector. Appropriately for the city of P. T. Barnum, one of the main attractions in the show is a circus tent with a ringmaster pulling a rabbit out of a hat, a clown, and circus animals. The western scene—cowboys and Indians and a stagecoach—is popular with the little ones, too. The show opens after Thanksgiving and runs through the first week in January.

The *Hartford Holiday Light Fantasia* lights up Goodwin Park on the Hartford-Wethersfield line. The show, produced by businessman Frank Marotta, started off with a few bumps in the road, but by its second year seemed to have ironed these out. Twenty-six displays are spread throughout the park, including Harry Potter's Magical Voyage, Husky Mania, a tribute to the UConn national champions, and UConn Field Goal, in which eighteen computerized footballs cross a field and light up the goalpost saying GO UCONN. The show starts the night before Thanksgiving and runs through Three King's Day in January. A portion of the proceeds goes to the Connecticut Children's Medical Center.

O Little Town

The Christmas spirit settles peacefully over Bethlehem, Connecticut. Except at the post office, that is, which is busier than Santa's North Pole workshop.

From January through November this may be just zip code 06751, but for the next twenty-four days, it's Christmas Central. In the first eleven months of the year, the post office handles about 250,000 pieces of mail. In the four weeks from Thanksgiving until Christmas, clerks process another 250,000 pieces, mostly cards from folks anxious to have their holiday greetings postmarked BETHLEHEM, THE CHRISTMAS TOWN.

Doris Nicholls is a former president of the historic society. She says, "We are one of fourteen towns in the United States called Bethlehem, and some of them don't even have post offices. In this area we are sought after. We love having the people come in, and especially we love having people use the cachets."

The cachets are special rubber stamps with holiday designs that this post office has offered customers every year since 1938. It began with postmaster Earl Johnson, who had a touch of Santa in his soul.

Postmaster Joan Manzi says, "He decided that he would like to send a Christmas card with a decorative seal, and he designed one. He paid for it out of his own pocket and it's been a tradition ever since."

These days local artists, postal employees, and even schoolchildren enter their designs in a contest held each October. A committee chooses the winner, and by Thanksgiving the new cachet is added to the collection in the boxes in the lobby.

Joan remembers stamping holiday cards here when she was a little girl. Some of her customers have been coming even longer than that.

Adela Parmelee has lived in Bethlehem nearly fifty years. "My husband is from Bethlehem and his family has come here ever since the post office has been here."

Others are newer to the tradition, like five-year-old Dmitry and his twin brother, Yuri, who are energetically stamping everything in sight, including each other.

Three-year-old Shannon Vescera is a veteran, according to her mom, Maureen. "She's been helping me ever since she could hold a stamper."

Customers arrive by the carload and sometimes the busload from all over the state—and sometimes from much farther away. Virginia Moody brought her cards from Pensacola, Florida. She carefully matches the cachet to her envelope's design, pronouncing the effect "just *too* good!"

Sally Cullen, a postal clerk for nine years, is decked out in a holiday sweatshirt. Despite working seven days a week this time of year, she says, "It's great to see the people come in. They come year after year as a holiday tradition and they spend the afternoon stamping their cards and having a really special holiday moment. I really enjoy it, and the time just passes really quickly. Before you know it, the three weeks are gone."

You might wonder if the rest of the year seems a little dull after the Christmas rush. "Yes," smiles one of the clerks, "but we need eleven months to rest up after this!"

If you'd like to get in on the Christmas cheer but can't make your way to Bethlehem, the postmaster will help. Send your addressed, stamped cards in a parcel to the post office, and the clerks will postmark them for you and send them on, at no extra charge. This year people sent cards from twenty-six states and five foreign countries.

It all adds up to a special feeling of Yuletide pride in this corner of the state, according to Maureen Vescera, who lives in Bethlehem. "It's the best small town in Connecticut. This is the true meaning of Christmas."

The Bethlehem Festival

The popularity of the post office's Christmas tradition led Bethlehem to capitalize on its Christmas cachet with a town festival. A little more than twenty years ago, when the town's Memorial Hall burned down, the festival was started as a way to raise money to build a new hall. It's usually held the first Friday and Saturday in December and features the lighting of a ninety-foot-tall tree on the town green, live music from carolers and bell choirs, and the arrival of Santa. The post office extends its hours to accommodate festivalgoers. Visitors can sample roasted chestnuts, take horse-drawn hayrides through town, visit the historic Bellamy-Ferriday House, and browse the work of dozens of crafters offering Christmas novelty items, quilts, toys, stained glass, ceramics, and more. The annual limited-edition pewter Christmas Town ornament is for sale.

Holiday downtowns have their own special magic. Clockwise from upper left: Chester, Madison, Litchfield, Mystic, Greenwich, Westport, Stonington, Guilford.

The Town of Bethlehem's manger and majestic tree. Right: Inside the church of the Abbey of Regina Laudis, a tree is covered with handmade birds.

Come to the Manger

At the Abbey of Regina Laudis in Bethlehem, Christmas is sacred.

Mother Margaret Georgina, one of forty Benedictine nuns who live at the monastery, says it's more than their faith that dictates this. It's also their location. "As it happens, we were founded here," she says. "We didn't expect to be founded in Bethlehem, so the fact that the Lord brought us here, we feel, is no accident."

The Lord brought their foundress to Bethlehem in 1947 as the result of a promise she made following the devastation of World War II. Vera Duss was an American who lived in France, became a doctor, and then entered the Abbey of Jouarre, becoming Mother Benedict Duss O.S.B. The Nazis occupied the abbey during the war. When General George Patton liberated the Abbey of Jouarre, Mother Benedict resolved to found a monastery in the United States in honor of Patton and his soldiers. Her vision became reality when a devout Connecticut Congregationalist named Robert Leather donated land to the Benedictine sisters, as a place for people to find solace in faith. The sisters farm some four hundred acres. They monitor its woodlands.

"The land isn't for us. It is here as a place for people to be able to come from anywhere," Mother Margaret Georgina explains. "We hope that there's a climate that makes them able to pray and to listen and to get a new perspective. So the land is for many more than us, we hope."

Stewardship of the land is part of the mission of the Benedictines, but their lives are regulated by their devotion to prayer. Still, they are intertwined. According to Mother Praxedes, "The land informs our prayer, and our prayer informs the way we work on the land."

Once in the middle of the night, and seven times throughout the day, a bell summons them to chapel. In Latin they sing the Divine Office as handed down by Saint Benedict fourteen hundred years ago. They are believed to be the only community of women in the United States pledged to preserve the ancient Gregorian chant.

They do it, according to Mother Margaret Georgina, because "when we were founded we were asked by Pope Paul VI to keep the Latin, which we've done. He said no matter what goes

on, the church has her language and someone has to keep it living. And so we keep that and we chant that."

Mother Margaret Georgina explains why she chose this life: "I came here at eighteen and I felt something extremely special and radiant here. I've actually found truth here that I couldn't turn away from."

The sisters live a contemplative life behind walls and enclosures, cloistered, for the most part, from the rest of the world. Yet they are commanded by the rule of Saint Benedict to offer hospitality. Though they worship behind a grill, the public is welcome for Mass and vespers. The Christmas tree in their small chapel is decorated with fused glass ornaments made by children under the guidance of Mother Praxedes, the resident artist. "It's amazing working with children how much freer they are than adults. They're so excited about seeing all the colors that they just start making compositions and making designs and then putting them together."

In their barnlike Church of Jesu Fili Mariae, an evergreen is the perch for more than forty varieties of birds handmade by Mother Praxedes. "The inspiration was members of the community. What birds would they be like?"

She painstakingly crafted more than one hundred birds from papier-mâché and real feathers, but called it a pleasure. "You can see the whole world in a feather! It's astounding how within one feather there's so much life."

The nuns sell Christmas trees and wreaths in a hut. In the Monastic Art Shop, ornaments and their two music CDs are for sale. Many come to see their magnificent crèche, believed to be a rare example of the art of Neapolitan crèche makers of the eighteenth century. The nativity scene is housed in a stable of the same vintage that once belonged to Joseph Bellamy, who opened the nation's first seminary nearby.

At the Abbey of Regina Laudis, visitors discover and celebrate the true meaning of Christmas in an inspiring setting. For more than fifty years, it has been a place to which the Benedictines have made a special commitment. According to Mother Margaret Georgina, the nuns take a vow of stability. "That means that we are vowed to this people. We are vowed to Bethlehem, Connecticut. It's very specific. It's not Idaho, it's not Michigan, it's Connecticut."

Christmas by Lantern Light

A fir tree is lashed to the mast of the *L. A. Dunton.* It is Christmas Eve 1876 in Mystic Seaport. Christmas is a time for fantasy, and once you step through the gates of the Seaport and into the nineteenth century, the magic begins.

A costumed guide takes our group of about a dozen into a time when America has just celebrated its one hundredth birthday with the Centennial Exposition in Philadelphia. The presidential election between Samuel Tilden and Rutherford B. Hayes is in dispute. It's Yuletide in the seaport village.

"Life in the nineteenth century has many fewer traditions than we have today," says our guide, who goes by the name Elizabeth Shaw Edwards. If we follow in the light of her lantern, we will observe and participate in some of the customs of an earlier time.

Elizabeth, dressed in the long skirts and petticoats of the nineteenth century, turns to a woman in our tour group and comments on her corduroy slacks. "Ma'am, I notice you're only wearing pantaloons. Where are you from?"

"I'm from Mystic, ma'am," the tourist responds.

"Ah, you must be from the other side of the river!" Elizabeth jokes, and the group laughs.

Our first stop is aboard the fishing schooner *L. A. Dunton,* where the crew is spending Christmas Eve preparing for its next voyage to the West Indies. "We want to make sure everything is shipshape for our upcoming voyage," explains first mate Angus Weller. "Let's see, here are the charts, our line, a weatherglass, and a sextant. You folks who travel by land-based conveyances have your signposts, mileposts, roads, and your maps to guide you on your way. But on a seagoing voyage pretty much any stretch of ocean looks like any other stretch of ocean. Without the proper equipment to guide us, we'd have no way of telling where we are."

Ahead of us, a light is burning as we make our way down the wharf. Although it's Christmas Eve, Lars Sanderson, the shipsmith, is laboring in his workshop. He pauses for a visit and a bit of gossip about a young lady who has returned home from Philadelphia, determined to stop her prearranged marriage.

This evening's merriment is based on a play by S. Annie Frost published in 1876 in *Godey's Lady's Book,* according to its director. "An orphaned young lady by the name of Lucy McGuire is adopted by her uncle," Chris Dobbs explains. "He has her best interest at heart and actually fits her into a prearranged marriage with the son of his business partner, who is William Buckingham. William Junior and Lucy have been betrothed since they were little kids. But for the last ten years both of them have been away. They come back to Mystic, each one not wanting to marry the other. So our story picks up there!"

Along the way we visit a lonely sailor in the Seaman's Friends hall who plays his fiddle, and we all dance a reel. Marc Bernier, who works in the shipyard maintaining the historic vessels, plays the sailor, Jake Jacobs. "I've been doing this for a number of years now," says Marc. "This gets me into the Christmas spirit. I love it."

We stop to sing carols on our way to the meetinghouse for the Christmas pageant, and there's a discussion of holiday traditions, old

and new. Elizabeth asks our group, "For Christmas dinner, do you have turkey or roast beef or ham? I understand that roasts and hams are traditions that come to us from England, but turkey and candied yams and cranberry sauce are all traditions that come from our good country, America. They don't even grow cranberries in England!"

At the finest house in the village, Mrs. McGuire, Lucy's grandmother, welcomes us with a batch of cookies, while her granddaughters decorate the tree with little American flags and paper cutouts. In 1876 Christmas trees are still a fairly new custom in America.

Mrs. McGuire has lighted a candle in each window "to remind us not to repeat the mistake of the innkeeper who turned away Joseph and Mary. When you have candles in your window, it means you're willing to welcome strangers. When the strangers see the light, they know they can come in and take shelter if they need it."

Soon we arrive at the meetinghouse. As we gather for the pageant and mingle with women in long skirts and bonnets and with gentlemen in fur hats, Kris Kringle arrives in a hooded cape.

Lucy beseeches her uncle to let her break the engagement: "Oh uncle, we have much to discuss now that I have returned. I won't marry just anybody just because I am told to!"

Outside the meetinghouse we hear the clattering of hooves as John Allegra arrives in an antique trolley pulled by a team of Percheron draft horses. As our little group scrambles aboard, John notes that Mystic Seaport takes on a special air in December after dark. "If we get a little snow, it gets everybody in the spirit. It's Christmas at Mystic Seaport every night this time of year."

As the trolley deposits us back at the Seaport gates, eight-year-old Lindsay Kenyon from New London pronounces Christmas better in the days gone by, "because they didn't have all these TVs and stuff."

Joshua Barrett says the lantern-light tour "gave me a good sense of going back in time and what it would've been like back then. I think Christmas celebrations were more sincere back then."

Marc Vakassian is an actor preparing to play Angus Weller the next evening. "From an acting standpoint, it's a lot of fun. From the historical perspective, it's just amazing to step back in time—and you really do. Even when we're between tours, we find ourselves talking in character as people come in and go out. You sometimes lose who you really are until it's over!"

And so does the audience. That's the magic of Mystic Seaport's Christmas Lantern Light Tours.

The gospel choir production of Black Nativity by the Alliance Theater of New Haven. At right, angels beam with joy at a nativity pageant in Rowayton.

Make a Joyful Noise

What a wonderful musical score has been written over the ages to accompany Christmas! When I came to Connecticut, I reveled in the holiday music that surrounded me. From my first apartment in downtown New Haven, I could walk to the legendary Woolsey Hall on the Yale campus and hear the finest choirs from around the state, and across the world, perform sacred and secular holiday music. A church established 350 years ago, Center Church on the Green, became the stage

for an award-winning gospel choir that raised the rafters with a performance of *Black Nativity*. I've never thought of Christmas carols in quite the same way again. At Trinity Church on the Green, the Christmas Eve midnight services are a revered century-old tradition marked by the angelic voices of the Boys Choir. One block from the place I called home, midnight Mass is sung in Polish, the language of my grandmother; three blocks away in Wooster Square, it's sung in Italian.

Choral music has always been a big part of the season for me. My mother sang in our church choir, and when I attended the School of the Holy Child in Suffern, New York, we gathered every Friday morning for school singing. It was a school requirement, and a joy. Blending voices, harmonizing, school singing taught us how to work and live together.

All over Connecticut chorales, choirs, orchestras, chamber groups, and bands of every description fill the air with Christmas music, from the glory of *Messiah* at the Bushnell to the medieval merriment at Connecticut College's Make We Joy concert, based on Olde English Christmas revels that celebrate the winter solstice. Tubas triumph in an annual concert in Essex. And then there's Siggy the singing dachshund, a singular performer, the likes of whom we may never see again.

There is music in Christmas for everyone. Even our pageants and parades include time for a community carol sing. It is truly the time of year to make a joyful noise!

Poetry and Prayer

Gospel music has a certain power—the power to make people get on their feet and clap and sing and shout "hallelujah." Raise a joyful noise, the Bible says, and the joyful sounds of gospel raise the rafters at the University of New Haven during the annual Alliance Theater production of Black Nativity.

The production brings together outstanding singers from churches all over Bridgeport to perform the "gospel song-play" penned by the great poet of the Harlem renaissance, Langston Hughes.

Carol Penney founded the Alliance Theater and has directed Black Nativity for nearly twenty years. The first act is titled "The Child Is Born." "It's the story of the nativity told with Langston Hughes's poetry," she says. "He has two beautiful poems in this particular section."

Narrators Gloria Richardson and Mekah-el Ben Israel delight in those words. They perform the verse in call and response, describing the Virgin Mary's thoughts about her newborn Son.

Mekah-el has played the narrator since the first Alliance Theater production of Black Nativity. "Taking Langston Hughes's words, which are so beautiful in the first place, and making them come alive is a special kind of task. His language, his ideas, the fact that he was a black man living in an America that is quite different from the America we live in now, exposed him to different kinds of things. He was one of the Harlem renaissance artists trying to bring some new ideas about culture to an America that had its own ideas at that time."

New ideas, but an age-old message, according to Gloria. "We try to let people know that Christ was born and was born for everyone, rich, poor, high, low, black, white. We want everyone to come together for this production. That's the wonder of it. Christ was born and He was born for all the world to see and that's what we try to put forth every year."

The first act blends traditional Christmas carols with gospel songs like "My Way's Cloudy," "Sweet Little Jesus Boy," and "Jesus the Light of the World," which the choir sings as the Christmas story unfolds.

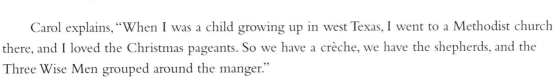

> *We'll walk in the light*
> *The beautiful light*
> *Come where the dewdrops of mercy shine bright*
> *Shine all around us by day and by night*
> *Jesus the light of the world.*
> *Hark the herald angels sing*
> *Jesus the light of the world*
> *Glory to the newborn king*
> *Jesus the light of the world.*

Carol explains, "When I was a child growing up in west Texas, I went to a Methodist church there, and I loved the Christmas pageants. So we have a crèche, we have the shepherds, and the Three Wise Men grouped around the manger."

And as they gather, a soloist leads the choir in a spiritual.

> *While shepherds kept their watching*
> *Over silent flocks by night*
> *Behold throughout the heavens*
> *There shone a holy light.*
> *Somebody ought to*
> *Go tell it on the mountain*
> *Over the hills and everywhere*
> *Go tell it on the mountain*
> *That Jesus Christ is born.*

The second act, which Hughes titled "The Word Is Spread," is less formal and more improvisational. Carol says the poet had a story to tell. "From two thousand years ago, from the birth of Christ, here's what American blacks have accomplished in terms of their church and their spirituality. This play is about that, the connection of people with each other."

As some cast members mingle with the audience, a modern-day prayer meeting takes shape on stage. Gloria takes the pulpit. Half singing, half preaching, she intones, "Now we're His worshipers and the Bible says we need to make a joyful noise. . . ."

The choir answers, "Amen!"

Gloria continues, louder this time, "I said a joyful noise!"

It is clear the faith of the cast members inspires their performances. "In the second half of the show you're in that church and the spirit actually comes at different times and you can't stop it and it's just a wonderful thing," says Gloria. That spirit moves the cast, and shapes the performance in different ways each night. Gloria continues, "They really think about what God

has done for them, that Jesus was born for them. We try to really let them know that that's what it's all about."

Mekah-el says for the cast, and for the audience, this is more than theater. "It is church to them; it is a church experience for them," he explains. "It's very similar to what you might find on a Sunday morning right here in towns like New Haven all across the country. This is black church at its finest. It's what many people are raised on from when they're little."

Playing a preacher in the second act, he exhorts the worshipers, "Show us how to turn our eyes to God." There's a chorus of amens.

Mekah-el continues, "Show the nation how to beat their swords into plowshares. That's why He came! Say amen! Say hallelujah!" There's a louder chorus of amens and hallelujahs. Once more he shouts, "Say amen! Say hallelujah!" The choir shouts and sings, "Amen!" One woman breaks into an impromptu dance.

For some in the audience, it is a new experience, Mekah-el says. "For those who have been raised in a tradition like Roman Catholicism, which is fairly staid, to see people jump up and shout for joy, that's an entirely different perception of how religion is pursued, how you feel your faith."

And he adds, "The most segregated hour in America is the religious time on Sundays. That's what we've got to breach, and this play helps us do that. It brings people together, and not just Christians. A lot of different kinds of people come to see this show."

Many will come back next year. "Over the years people have left the theater saying to us how they finally have the spirit of Christmas, because of the show bringing back the idea that it's not just buying presents and Christmas trees and lights, but it's the real essence of sharing, sharing in the season. That's something that you can't put a premium on, something quite beautiful."

Gloria adds, "We involve the audience so much. We get them into the music and the clapping and everything that goes on. They have such a good time. If they came in with a problem or feeling down or whatever, when they leave it's all gone. It's just a completely different feeling altogether. They leave here joyous."

Joyous and filled with the spirit that is Christmas.

Live Nativities

Live nativity scenes are enacted all over Connecticut. The Valley Brook Community Church in Granby, for instance, presented its first at Salmon Brook Park. For two hours on a Saturday night in December in costumes borrowed from a local church, the twenty-five actors braved frigid fifteen-degree temperatures. Luminaria led visitors to the manger scene inside a park bandshell. Live animals, including a donkey, sheep, goats, and chickens from Simsbury's Fleming Farms, added a touch of reality to the tableau. Visitors called the scene powerful, and some stopped to kneel by the manger, despite the cold. "This is our gift to the community, which we're proud to be part of," Pastor Clark Pfaff said.

In another corner of the state, Rowayton has all the charm of small-town Connecticut, but it's actually a section of one of Connecticut's larger cities, Norwalk. This waterfront "village" (as it considers itself) embraces community events, whether it's a summertime parade or the children's nativity pageant at Christmas.

The nativity pageant dates back to the sad days following the assassination of President Kennedy in 1963. Rowayton resident Putsey Ritchey and her neighbors wanted to do something to bring the community together and raise its spirits. They scrambled that year to assemble the nativity pageant.

Today the pageant has a nearly forty-year history and involves many segments of the community. Held outdoors at the Rowayton School field, it features Girl Scouts portraying angels and Boy Scouts as the Three Wise Men and their contingent, while Little Leaguers may suit up as shepherds. Some children who have grown up and gone off to college still participate in the pageant when they come home for the holidays. The program is ecumenical, with readings by a Catholic priest, a Methodist minister, and clergy from the United Church of Rowayton. There is only one performance, generally held on a weekend evening, in mid-December.

Above: The nativity pageant in Rowayton. Left: A young shepherd tends the flock at the Valley Brook Christmas pageant in Granby.

33

Trees in the Rigging

Santa may make his rounds by sleigh in most places, but in the picturesque river town of Essex, the jolly old elf arrives at Steamboat Dock by boat. He's escorted by ships with riggings dressed in holiday lights and colorful nautical flags. Santa is then welcomed with a parade in an annual event known as Trees in the Rigging.

A platoon of antique cars leads off the parade, which begins at town hall. The Sailing Masters of 1812 Fife and Drum Corps, the Sea Scouts, and an antique fire truck are close behind. Caroling townspeople follow, many carrying period candle lanterns. The Deep River Junior Ancient Fife and Drum Corps brings up the rear as the procession winds through town to

Steamboat Dock. Along the way, historic characters from Essex Christmases past—including Lieutenant William Pratt, a well-known seventeenth-century shipowner—join the parade. It all ends up at the wharf, where Santa visits with the children and everyone sips hot cider provided by the Griswold Inn.

The Connecticut River Museum stays open into the early evening, featuring a holiday exhibit that reflects the maritime history of Essex. Five hundred sailing vessels were built in Essex, including the *Oliver Cromwell,* Connecticut's first battleship, which was launched in 1775.

Essex has been called the Best Small Town in America, and its community spirit, evident in the twenty-year tradition of Trees in the Rigging, is one of the reasons why.

Christmas City of Connecticut

"Never have we seen such brilliant and effective city and home decorations in any city. That this should prevail so soon after Norwich was devastated by flood and hurricane is an amazing example of the courage of the people." That's what the judges of holiday decorations in Norwich said in 1938, after declaring the winners of the city's home-decorating contest. It's that spirit that made Norwich the Christmas City of Connecticut, a title it captured several times in the years leading up to World War II in a competition that included as many as eight other cities.

Kathy Relyea had heard tales of how the city outdid itself in holiday displays in the 1920s and '30s and how the "canopy of lights" over Franklin Square and the light-bedecked gingerbread of Norwich City Hall attracted shoppers and tourists from as far away as New Hampshire and Pennsylvania. In the late 1980s she kicked off a campaign to light up city hall once again. It took five years to accomplish, but Norwich now twinkles and glows each winter, thanks to Kathy—fondly known as the Christmas Lady of Norwich.

The annual lighting of city hall the day after Thanksgiving signals the start of the Norwich Winter Festival, which stretches almost until Christmas Day and includes a Wacky Hat contest for people and their pets, sale of a specially designed commemorative ornament, Nutcracker on Ice at

Norwich's "Canopy of Lights" revival began in 1996 and now spreads throughout downtown.

the municipal skating rink, and the citywide house-decorating contest. The highlight is the Norwich Winter Festival parade, which takes place the afternoon of the second Sunday after Thanksgiving and features floats, fire engines, horse-drawn carriages, marching bands, scouts, shriners, swing dancers, and, of course, the arrival of Santa Claus.

Franklin Square (top) and the Laurel Hill Bridge, Norwich, aglow in 1937.

Holiday on Parade

Holiday spirit is on the march in Connecticut in a tradition that goes back to Colonial times: a wintertime parade. The *Christmas Torchlight Parade and Muster* has been held for thirty years in Old Saybrook, but it harks back three hundred years or more. According to local historians, in early America the local militia would muster and march to the village green with their fifes and drums, usually in early December. When the townspeople heard the music, they would rush from their homes, carrying torches and lanterns, and follow the militia. The tradition was revived three decades ago in Old Saybrook, and the parade now attracts about forty Ancient Fife and Drum Corps and a host of other marching units. Spectators carry torches, lanterns, and sometimes even flashlights. As the last parade unit passes, the crowd falls in behind them for the Community Carol Sing.

The Colonial Saybrook Fifes and Drums sponsor the festivities. The Fifth Connecticut Volunteer Infantry is the official escort unit. The Christmas Torchlight Parade takes place the second Saturday in December at 6:00 P.M., regardless of weather. In fact, some of the hearty Yankees in town say the worse the weather, the bigger the crowds!

One of Connecticut's newest holiday parades lights up Groton in December. Started just three years ago, the *Groton White Lights Holiday Parade* follows the "Miracle Mile" through the business district. At the end of the parade, Santa lights the community tree, and everyone joins in a carol sing. Trophies are awarded to the best floats and marching units. Organizers of the parade say they hope the annual event will unite the community.

The *Montville Holiday Light Parade* is another relative newcomer in the parade category, but residents say the event is growing. Most of the marchers are scouts, though the fire department has come up with some imaginative entries, including a fire truck done up to look like a house on fire. The parade heads down Route 32 through town at dusk on the first Sunday in December.

Top: Parading in Hartford on Three Kings Day. Bottom: Rudolph the red-nosed tractor at the Christmas Torchlight Parade in Old Saybrook.

Two surfers from California, relocated to the waterfront village of Niantic, brought with them the idea for one of the most popular holiday events in southeastern Connecticut. The *Niantic Light Parade* steps off down Main Street just after dark on the second Sunday in

December. Every entry in the parade is lighted, whether it be an elaborate float resembling a carousel, a helicopter that really goes up and down, or an eighty-foot-long train carrying animated teddy bears. Marching Brownie scouts sport strands of battery-operated lights; musicians in the marching band light their instruments; some marchers string lights on their horses and llamas. Spectators light their caps. Twelve thousand people have been known to show up for the spectacle, and window seats at Constantine's Restaurant are so popular the owner auctions them off to the highest bidder. All the money goes to help needy families over the holidays.

Top left and right: Proudly marching in Old Saybrook's Torchlight Parade. Bottom left: Horse-drawn hayrides are part of Wallingford's Season of Celebration. Right: A snowman rides a float at the Niantic Light Parade

Wallingford's historic town center is the setting for *Season of Celebrations*. Santa and Mrs. Claus preside from the town hall foyer, all decked out for the holidays. Local celebrities stroll about dressed in Victorian costume. The First Congregational Church hosts a luncheon and crafts fair, and professional ice carvers compete for cash prizes on the parade ground. Elves in little elf houses dispense treats to good little girls and boys. A brass quartet entertains, and visitors pile into horse-drawn carriages. After the children's chorus sings carols in front of town hall, Frosty the Snowman leads the kids, all carrying jingle bells, in a merry procession down Center Street. Santa and Mrs. Claus arrive at Johanna Manfreda Fishbein Park in a white carriage, where they light the town tree at dusk. The all-day festivities take place on the first Saturday in December.

Siggy Sings

One of the most sociable shopping events of the holiday season is the annual stroll in the charming shoreline town of Old Saybrook. Whether it's sixty degrees or freezing outside, crowds come out to enjoy special activities ranging from a wreath sale to a spaghetti supper to horse-drawn wagon rides on Main Street. Nearly every merchant offers refreshments, and many showcase entertainers.

Without a doubt, the star of the stroll for a decade was Siggy. The singing and keyboard-playing dachshund hung up his Santa suit in 2000, but for ten years he packed them in at the Paint Shop, giving performances every half hour. Siggy's owner-agent Erma Gimbel figures the pooch picked up some of his musical abilities watching her son, a professional keyboardist who toured with Aerosmith and Foreigner. As the *Hartford Courant* noted in an editorial marking Siggy's retirement, "For those who have never heard the stylings of Siggy, the singing dog of Old Saybrook, the time is sadly past. Another of life's unseized opportunities slips away." There are those who hope Ol' Brown Eyes won't be able to ignore the allure of his fans, and will make a return appearance. With or without Siggy, the Saybrook Stroll happens the first Friday night in December.

Standing Ovation

Hearing Handel's *Messiah* performed by the Hartford Chorale and Hartford Symphony Orchestra in the concert hall at the Bushnell is one of the most moving experiences of the holiday season, but standing on the stage and singing it is even better. Opened in 1930, the beautiful art deco concert hall was designed by the architectural firm that would later design New York's Radio City Music Hall.

Tony Senatore, a member of the Hartford Chorale for more than ten years, has sung for the queen at Westminster Abbey and in concert halls across Europe. Still, he says singing at the Bushnell is a thrill. "The Bushnell has this old-time ambience, and it's wonderful to perform in front of nearly three thousand people," he says. "And the acoustics are wonderful."

The Hartford Chorale's members come from many walks of life and from all over Connecticut, some from New York and Massachusetts. The all-volunteer chorus of 150 is selected annually through competitive audition. Director Henley Denmead sets a high standard for the singers, and they work hard to meet it, devoting at least one evening a week to rehearsals and spending plenty of time at home learning the music. What motivates them to work this hard?

"Some people play softball, some sing!" says Joan Gurski, a soprano from West Hartford who has sung with the chorale for a decade. "Singing in general is a source of both joy and stress relief for me. It is my respite. The joy of choral music is in the balance and blending of voices and the opportunity to perform some of the greatest works ever written by some of the greatest composers who ever lived."

Composers like George Frideric Handel, who wrote *Messiah* in 1741. It is still among the most beloved and powerful of choral works. The Hartford Chorale and Hartford Symphony Orchestra have performed the oratorio annually since 1972, and theirs is one of the most acclaimed versions in southern New England. One major reason is Henley Denmead.

"Every year, people ask me how I can continue to find something new in this piece, some reason to keep on doing it every year," says Henley, who has led the group since its beginning and conducted all but three of the annual *Messiah* performances. "Handel's music has that special energy and power that never fails to lift and rejuvenate the human spirit."

The singers agree. "When you have the responsibilities of a family and a job, you have to choose how to spend your limited personal time carefully," says Tony, the father of two sons. "I choose chorale because singing is good for the heart, and good for the soul. Singing is nourishing."

"This year's performance had a special energy I've never felt in previous *Messiahs*," Joan adds.

"The truth is, the singers themselves become reenergized each year," observes Henley.

And they are devoted to their director. Some have worked with him since his days as music professor at Central Connecticut State University.

Henley makes sure the chorale knows *Messiah* almost as well. The oratorio is based on scripture from both the Old and New Testaments. It contains the choruses "And the Glory of the Lord" and "For Unto Us a Child Is Born." For many the highlight is the immortal "Hallelujah" chorus, a chorus that so moved King George II in its premiere London performance that the king leapt to his feet to applaud. When the king stands, everyone stands, so a tradition of standing for the "Hallelujah" was begun and continues to this day. Music historians believe it was the world's first standing ovation for any performance. Despite this, Henley Denmead says, "*Messiah* did not enjoy the popularity of many of Handel's other oratorios during the composer's lifetime."

Some 250 years later, *Messiah* is one of the most popular pieces of sacred music with audiences and with the Hartford Chorale, which has performed many other works. "It is truly an emotional favorite for all of us," says chorale president Dougla Pyrke. An emotional favorite and Connecticut holiday tradition.

The Colonial Concert

The music and the setting are both perfect at Orchestra New England's Colonial Concert, a holiday tradition for more than twenty years. Attired in eighteenth-century finery, the orchestra performs in the meetinghouse of one of New Haven's historic churches on the green. The United Church of Christ congregation was formed in 1742 when members separated from the established church in New Haven. Not long after, Joseph Haydn wrote his magnificent *Oxford* symphony, no. 92, which Orchestra New England now performs in its annual "Concert of Mufick." This is a concert the Founding Fathers of our nation might have enjoyed—and in a setting where they would feel at home. The church is festooned for Christmas and lighted by candles. With a strong tradition of fine music, the United Church of Christ is home to a pipe organ, three grand pianos, and an Italian harpsichord. Conductor and orchestra founder Jim Sinclair plays his part costumed and coiffed in a powdered wig. Following the concert, mulled wine is served in the church hall, completing the atmosphere of a Colonial soiree.

Holiday performances add to the excitement of the season. The Santa Lucia Festival, held since 1910 at Emanuel Lutheran Church in Hartford, celebrates the beginning of Swedish Christmas (top right and bottom left). Make We Joy at Connecticut College includes fire eaters, elves, and holiday song (top left, center left, and bottom right). The tuba concert in Essex is an unforgettable experience (center right).

Sights and Sounds of Christmas

More than fifty thousand people have been given a beautiful gift by the Black Rock Congregational Church in Fairfield over the last seventeen years—a concert and pageant known as the Sights and Sounds of Christmas. This performance of secular and sacred music is so popular that the church is filled to capacity for each of its nine annual performances. The show opens with remarkable stagecraft that includes toy soldiers marching and a young girl actually ice skating as the outstanding choir and orchestra perform holiday favorites. The audience joins in for a carol sing. When the stage lights come back up, the one-hundred-member choir, now in formal attire and framed by candlelight, tells the story of the life of Christ through music, drama, and scripture readings in an original program compiled by the Reverend James Marshall. The elaborately staged

multimedia presentation goes beyond the nativity to reveal Christ's resurrection and ascension into Heaven.

Reverend Marshall, known as Pastor Jim by the congregation, began the production shortly after his arrival at Black Rock in 1984. There were only two shows scheduled for that first year, but so many people turned out on the second and last night that they added a "command performance" for that very same evening. Pastor Jim calls the concert "a gift to the community," and says, "I want people to experience the true meaning of Christ. Not to see it or hear it, but to experience it, to feel it in their souls."

Almost all the performers are church members, not professional artists, but their musicianship and dedication are exceptional. One year a severe winter storm caused flooding in the area. Although one of the soloists had to be rescued by firemen that afternoon, she sang to a full house in church that evening.

Performances are the first and second weekends in December. Tickets to the Sights and Sounds of Christmas are free, but the church asks that you bring a contribution of nonperishable food, which is donated to the area needy. By the last of the nine performances, the church hall is invariably stuffed with a mountain of canned goods!

Symphony on Ice

Santa gets a lot of help in the toy department from the U.S. Marine Corps Toys for Tots program, which hands out thousands of toys to kids in need all over Connecticut. The biggest single gift-giving event in the state, and one of the largest in the nation, is United Technologies Symphony on Ice, held at the Hartford Civic Center in early December. This holiday skating and music performance features a glittering cast of international skating stars and Olympic medal winners, along with the music of the Hartford Symphony. Free tickets to the show are distributed through greater Hartford area libraries, but each person attending the event must donate one new unwrapped toy. More than a quarter million toys have been collected since the show began in 1980.

The Nutcracker

The Nutcracker is a holiday fairy tale told in ballet slippers. The story of a little girl's dream is customarily set in Germany. Hartford, however, has a tradition of nontraditional Nutcrackers.

American Nutcracker garnered national attention when it debuted there. The Hartford Ballet set the tale in the American Southwest during the gold rush of the 1800s. The music was still Tchaikovsky's classic score. Enid Lynn, the artistic director, described the ballet's transformation. "It's really more the scenic and visual elements that are different. There are some wonderful images that celebrate the flora and fauna of America."

American Nutcracker featured traditional sugarplum fairies and snowflakes, but there were honeybees, a giant spider, and a golden eagle, too. Sunflowers danced with butterflies. Some of the

fanfare over the production centered on the involvement of the Mashantucket Pequot Tribal Nation, which underwrote the ballet's development to the tune of half a million dollars.

During the 2000 holiday season, Dance Connecticut, a new organization allied with the Hartt School of the University of Hartford, premiered its own holiday ballet: *Nutcracker in a Nutshell*, a one-hour version of *The Nutcracker* choreographed by Adam Miller. His goal was to update the ballet to appeal to today's young audiences. "This fast-paced production, which includes elements from slapstick comedy to swashbuckling heroics, is really an exciting adventure story for children," said Miller, who grew up in a large family. He drew upon some favorite memories of his own childhood, including his love of the Marx Brothers and the Three Stooges. The sword scenes, he said, "come from memories of my own living room battles with my brothers."

Miller localized the tale, suggesting that *The Nutcracker* takes place in Connecticut. Scenery included a window in the drawing room with a view of the sea; Clara's father was dressed as a sea captain. The production features Dance Connecticut's professional dancers and students from the university's dance degree program. Nearly fifty children age eight to eighteen from the School of Dance Connecticut help put a special spin on a holiday classic.

Songs of Joy

Hearing the voices of angels? More likely it's one of Connecticut's own choral groups.

Paul Halley, a Grammy-winning composer, conductor, and performer, founded the Norfolk-based children's choir *Chorus Angelicus* in 1991 at the request of his own children, who had sung in cathedral choirs in New York City. Paul had been music director at the Cathedral of Saint John the Divine in Manhattan, the world's largest cathedral, and he had performed for almost two decades with the Paul Winter Consort. The family found serenity moving to the hamlet of Norfolk, but the children missed the music.

Today Halley directs fifty children from around the region in Chorus Angelicus, and twenty-five more comprise the training choir. The kids are dedicated, rehearsing twice a week for their schedule of concerts, which are held at churches around Connecticut and in places like Boston's Symphony Hall. Chorus Angelicus has issued two ethereal CDs that combine New Age

Chorus Angelicus performs.

music with traditional, sacred, and secular compositions. Its *Christmas Angelicus* CD was recorded in part at Saint Joseph's Cathedral in Hartford.

Chorus Angelicus has been performing for about a decade. The *Trinity Choir of Men and Boys,* on the other hand, has been an institution in New Haven for well over a century. The oldest continuous choir of men and boys in Connecticut, it was founded in 1885. Only six such choirs in the entire country are older. The choral group carries on a tradition that began in the Middle Ages. The Boys Choir is the "traveling team," giving concerts at Carnegie Hall, Boston's Symphony Hall, the National Cathedral, and the Metropolitan Museum of Art in addition to several European tours. The celebrated choral group has been a favorite at the White House, has worked with renowned conductor Robert Shaw, and has performed Leonard Bernstein's *Mass* with the composer in attendance. In 2000 the choir issued its first CD, *Christmas Around,* containing new and favorite music for Advent, Christmas, and Epiphany. Organist and choirmaster R. Walden Moore is planning a special season as Trinity Church celebrates its two hundred and fiftieth anniversary.

Trinity Boys Choir in concert at the White House.

Twelfth Night

On a Friday evening in January, big wet flakes of snow are falling gently as a line of people forms outside Hartford's landmark Asylum Hill Congregational Church. They are here for the annual Boar's Head and Yule Log Festival, an ancient processional celebrating the Epiphany, or twelfth day after Christmas. The commanding cathedral-like church was built of Portland brownstone in 1865; it once claimed Mark Twain as a member. Inside, the soaring nave is beribboned and garlanded in red and gold streamers and banners—and it seems a great banquet is about to begin. A chamber group, jugglers, rogues, puppeteers, and strolling singers entertain. A magician performs sleight of hand, acrobats somersault and cartwheel up and down the aisles, and the

audience chortles at a jester's tomfoolery with a dancing bear. Bagpipers enter the church, and the procession begins with a Highland dance. Trumpets herald the entrance of the king and queen and the lords and ladies as the choir sings, "The boar's head, as I understand, is the rarest dish in all this land."

The Boar's Head and Yule Log Festival is indeed a spectacle to behold, with a cast, choir, and orchestra of 225 people all elaborately costumed and choreographed and accompanied by live animals. In medieval England the boar was a symbol of evil, and serving the boar's head at Christmas was symbolic of Christ's triumph over Satan. The pageantry of the procession can be traced to Queens College in Oxford, where it began not long after the university was founded in 1340. Boar's-head festivals grew to be very popular at the great English manor houses in the seventeenth century. The custom was carried on in Colonial America—beginning in Connecticut, some say.

The procession in the Asylum Hill church delights the audience. Lords and ladies and King Wenceslas are followed by a great parade of cooks and staff, bearing all manner of food and offerings that include live squawking geese, doves cooing in cages, holly, and mistletoe. A punchbowl of steaming wassail is carried in, along with a giant mince pie and of course the boar's head, dressed in ribbons and a frilly cap and borne on a pallet. Traditional English carols are sung, with the audience joining in.

And then the church is plunged into darkness, and a sprite arrives with woodsmen bearing the Yule log. The Yule log symbolizes the rekindling of warmth and love and, in Christianity, has come to represent the love of Christ. Now the story of the nativity will be told, with Joseph and Mary arriving on a donkey. The angels and the shepherds tell their part of the Christmas story. The Magi arrive to adore the Christ child, bearing gold, frankincense, and myrrh, attended by servants and accompanied by llamas and a camel wearing a sequined saddlecloth.

From the audience there is an "oooooooh" as the beast bends its knees to fit beneath the arched doorway.

A small child carries a lighted candle into the darkened church, symbolizing the light of Christ coming into the world. The entire assembly kneels to worship in prayer and joyous song. Finally the Yule sprite returns, and the child and a monk carry forth the light into the world.

The first performance at Asylum Hill Congregational Church thirty-five years ago was a much smaller and simpler affair. The congregation recycled draperies and bathrobes into costumes that were a far cry from today's theatrical splendor. Grace Einsel baked and glazed the first fifty-

pound boar's head for nine hours in an oversized oven. (Today the head is a permanent prop, thanks to a taxidermist.) The original giant "mince" pie was stuffed with baked beans, cereal, and anything else that would give it the right look. Dick Einsel, the minister of music then, wondered if anyone would come to the sole performance. They did, and they are still coming. Today there are five performances each January, on the weekend closest to Epiphany, and the five thousand tickets are in great demand.

For pageantry, tomfoolery, folderol, and a great deal of music and entertainment, the Boar's Head Festival is king. It is also a moving telling of the reason for the season.

Deck the Halls

From the extreme to the exquisite, decorating is an essential element of the holidays. To me, the classic Colonial home with a slender white candle in each window, a wreath on the door, and evergreen roping along a picket fence says *Christmas in Connecticut* as clear as day. All that's needed is a dusting of snow to sparkle in the reflections of white lights strung in fir trees. It's no surprise that Martha Stewart found so much inspiration here in our corner of New England.

The settlers of our state, who came here to find religious freedom, didn't believe in festive celebrations of Christmas. Inquire at Mystic Seaport during their annual lantern-light tours about the earliest Christmases in Connecticut and you'll find there were no trees, no big dinners, and no gifts for the children. Connecticut was the first New England state to declare Christmas a legal holiday, but that didn't happen until 1845. Two hundred Christmases in Connecticut had already passed.

That would not have sat well with some people in Connecticut today, who deck the halls in a style so exuberant it lures visitors from miles around. The ritual of Christmas decorating begins just after Labor Day in eastern Connecticut, when Mervin Whipple begins work on his enormous and elaborate holiday display. It takes fourteen weeks to install nearly four hundred animated creatures and 108,000 lights (at last count!). In New Britain, Rita Giancola needs three months to put up all her holiday decorations. No wonder; it took thirty years to collect them all. When Rita opens her home to the public, it's to share the spirit and to help neighbors in need. Her admission charge is a donation of canned food, and her pantry has helped get several families through some hard times. As guests wander "oohing" and "ahhing" through Rita's display, they are likely to run into her husband, Al, having a cup of coffee in the kitchen. He's accustomed to the traffic and to his wife's inexhaustible enthusiasm for the holidays.

This is the time of year when family and friends are not the only guests warmed by the hearth. An old New England tradition says that a candle in the window welcomes anyone in need of shelter and a bit of cheer at Christmastide.

Left: A welcome glow in Stonington. Above: Rita Giancola's enthusiastic style of decorating, New Britain.

Mr. Whipple's Wonderland

In eastern Connecticut Christmas comes when Mervin Whipple flips a light switch. Well, a lot of light switches, to tell the truth. For more than thirty years, Mervin Whipple has been setting his corner of Killingly aglow in a monumental display of Christmas spirit. It takes fourteen weeks to set up and fourteen more weeks to take down the three-acre holiday extravaganza—and that's with help from the Masons, the Lions, and a local technical school.

"We try to start setting up the day after Labor Day," he explains. "And I mean not just a couple of hours a day. It means practically an eight-hour day, and sometimes twelve or fourteen hours when it gets nearer opening night. We have to test all these lights, too, before we throw the switch, because it'd be a very embarrassing situation if I put the switch on and they didn't all work."

That means testing 108,000 lights and 384 animated characters that dance, bow, wave, sing, and cavort to the delight of the visitors who line up outside Christmas Wonderland as soon as it gets dark. It's a lot of work, but Mervin loves sharing Christmas. That's why he had MR. CHRISTMAS embroidered on the red cutaway coat he had sewn in Singapore, the coat he wears every night of December as he greets each and every visitor.

"Hello, Merry Christmas!" he says in a hearty voice. Mr. Whipple smiles at babies, shakes hands, and even offers a few hugs as visitors stream through his door.

Over the years he has welcomed 1.3 million visitors. Mr. Whipple knows, because he counts each one. "This is my trademark right here," he says, holding up a small metal counter. "Every person who comes through the door, I click them off. That's how I keep track of my attendance." On a busy night that might mean shaking two thousand seven hundred hands. "I want to be sure that they know how much I appreciate them coming. So every one of them that I talk to, I say 'Merry Christmas' and I thank them for coming. That's what I do every night of the week."

And after they all go home, Mr. Christmas thinks of what he can do better next year. "My wife says I think of it too much and I don't think of her enough! But when I stand at the door, I try to think to myself, *How can I improve this? What can I add? What can I change next year?* The older I get, the harder it gets to be, 'cause my imagination is kind of failing, too."

You'd never know it. Skiing penguins and a teddy bear band are recent additions. "When I bought them they were stuffed bears, and when they landed in here we had to unstuff them, perform an autopsy on them," he laughs. "We took them apart and we added the motors. And then that wasn't enough. I had to add some costumes."

Most of the animated characters are custom-made for Mr. Whipple at a company in New Jersey. In display cases set up along stone paths crisscrossing a snow-frosted hillside, horses pull old-fashioned sleighs past a Victorian skating scene. Elves bake cookies and chipmunks fly airplanes.

Dave O'Connor, a visitor from Florida, had not seen Wonderland since he was a boy, more than twenty years earlier. He remembers how big and bright it all seemed. "When I was a kid, it was so overwhelming. It really wasn't that big then, but it seemed so. Now after all these years coming back up here, it's grown so much, it's overwhelming again!"

Deborah Rockefeller visits each Christmas. "Every year he adds more, and every year I see something different that I didn't get before. I think it's excellent what he does around here."

In a snug showroom that's usually Mr. Whipple's business storefront, children walk right up to seven-foot-tall fantasy figures swathed in silver and teal chiffon riding unicorns and twirling on a snowy dance floor. Overhead a train whistles as it circles the building.

Four-year-old Casey and nine-year-old Bria Bristol look around with wide eyes. "I like the train," says Casey. Bria is impressed with the wintry scenes: "I think it's very nice and I like all the statues that they have."

The showroom, so filled with smiles and laughter at Christmas,

usually houses Everlasting Memorials, Mr. Whipple's monument business. "I'm superintendent of cemeteries in the town of Killingly, and I run approximately two hundred funerals a year," he explains. "This is the only time of year when I can actually tell a person, 'It's nice to see you!' The rest of the year I have to say, 'I'm awful sorry for what has happened.' So this does bring joy to my life."

The kind of joy that only comes after experiencing grief. Christmas Wonderland is a memorial of sorts to Mervin's beloved stepson, who died in a tragic accident shortly after he returned home from Vietnam. Mervin and his stepson had set up a manger scene in front of their home and promised to make something even bigger together the next year. But that was not to be. Today, the manger is still here, and each year the display has grown bigger and bigger.

When Mervin Whipple opened Christmas Wonderland more than thirty years ago he vowed he would never charge admission. He never wanted a single person turned away because he or she couldn't afford to get in. He's kept that promise even though he thinks he's probably invested more than a million dollars in the display. The electric bill alone runs about four thousand dollars a season, but Mr. Whipple just laughs over it. "I got arrested last year because the electric meter was going over the speed limit, it was turning so fast," he jokes, adding, "We are pulling right now 233,000 watts."

But after all, he says, it's only money, and he's buried enough people to know you can't take it with you. He'd rather spread some joy, and that's why he relishes being known as Mr. Christmas. "They've called me that for more than twenty-five years. I intend to have it etched on my tombstone when I go home, and I mean that, too. Because it's been a great, great thing."

All Decked Out

"Merry Christmas from our house to your house" calls the outdoor speaker. From a block away you can feel and hear the Christmas spirit at the New Britain home of Rita and Al Giancola. Dozens of characters line the lawn and rooftop, and carols resound from the outside speakers. Inside, it's a sparkling Christmas fantasyland in every room.

I asked Rita whether she knows of anyone else who has ever put together such an elaborate display. Rita doesn't hesitate. "Not to my knowledge, no, and no one ever will."

She's probably right. She's been collecting thousands of decorations for decades. Putting them all up is a chore that takes almost three months. The theory that guides her decorating? If one Santa is good, fifteen are better. An army of animated figures inhabits the rooms, along with a dozen trees and miles of garland and lights.

To some with less Christmas spirit, it might look a little overdone. But not to Rita. "Oh, no. I see some spaces I have to fill." She may be the only one who does. From chandeliers to shower curtains, it seems that every square inch is decorated.

You're probably wondering what it's like to live in a house like this. Rita loves it, her son says he's gotten used to it, and her husband, Al, swears, "This has gotta be the last year. It has to be!"

But Al says that every year, and he doesn't really mean it, because visiting the house is a tradition for thousands of people. It started in the late 1970s, when Rita noticed passersby peeking into her windows. Now the Giancolas open their doors to the public for a few days each season. The admission charge is a donation of nonperishable food for a needy family. Some years they've collected almost sixty thousand cans of food and distributed them throughout New Britain. Although some of it goes to places like the shelter for battered women, some also goes to individual families Rita hears about. She donated enough food to one mother with cancer to feed her family all year.

And that, says Rita, is the true meaning of Christmas. "It means giving. We all do too much taking and not enough giving. People forget that Christ was born on Christmas Day. And they should think more of that."

In her festive way, Rita Giancola gives Christmas back its real meaning.

Decorations from the elegant to the exuberant, clockwise from upper left: Old Saybrook, Higganum, Old Wethersfield, Redding Ridge, Guilford, Westville, New Canaan.

Home for the Holidays

This is a hospitable time of year when many of us invite friends and family to visit. But imagine inviting several *thousand* people to traipse through your house to see your holiday decorations!

Holiday home tours are popular seasonal fund-raisers for churches, community organizations, and other charities. For twenty years, for instance, the *Friends of the Mark Twain House* have opened some of greater Hartford's most intriguing homes to visitors at the holidays. Six private homes— some of which qualify as mansions—and two historic house museums are included on the tour. Eight floral designers and nearly one hundred musicians set a festive tone. One of the museum homes, the Isham-Terry House, was designed in an Italian villa style in 1854 and has been carefully preserved. Still, the highlight of the tour (and its beneficiary) is the house where Mark

Twain (Samuel Clemens) and his family lived from 1874 to 1891. This nineteen-room mansion is where Twain penned such classics as *The Adventures of Tom Sawyer, Adventures of Huckleberry Finn,* and *A Connecticut Yankee in King Arthur's Court.* Louis Comfort Tiffany's design firm decorated the first floor of the house, which was somewhat

The Mark Twain House, with first-floor decorations by Louis Comfort Tiffany's design firm.

The Mark Twain House, left. Below and next page: At the Franco home in Cheshire.

controversial in its day. In 1874 the *Hartford Daily Times* called it "one of the oddest looking buildings in the state ever designed for a dwelling, if not in the whole country." But Twain described the house as having "a heart and a soul" and said "we could not enter unmoved." At Christmastime the house is decorated as though Clemens family members might step through the door to celebrate the holidays. The Hartford House Tour generally takes place on a Sunday early in December.

In Cheshire the *Church of the Epiphany* asks five families to open their homes for tours every other year, and tries to find homes that help illustrate Cheshire's history. Joe and Lisa Franco's historic home was built in 1815 as part of Dr. Thomas Tryon Cornwall's estate. Dr. Cornwall built the house for his carriage driver, and for a while it housed a pharmacy for the doctor's cancer patients. Lucille Williams, a previous owner, painted murals in the foyer depicting early Cheshire scenes, and Lisa's father, Nino Maurizi, lovingly restored them. Colonial, Victorian, country, and cottage antiques and accents are gracefully arranged throughout the house, and a committee of

volunteers created garlands and wreaths using raffia, berries, and other fruit, in keeping with the age and feeling of the home. The table by the fire is set for Christmas brunch. Antique ornaments dangle from feather trees, replicas of the first artificial trees, which were made from real goose feathers. Each home offers live music. Lunch is served at the parish center, and so are complimentary coffee and baked goods. A locally made quilt is raffled off, and Cheshire-grown poinsettias are for sale.

Not only do house tours give you a chance to peek inside homes you've probably passed by and wondered about, but they're also great for getting ideas for decorating. Local florists and decorators often let their imaginations run free as they create holiday displays that complement the unique qualities of the homes. That's what you'll find on the *Westport Historical Society* holiday tour, where five area florists create elaborate holiday decorations for some of the grandest homes on the "gold coast." This well-known tour is usually scheduled for the first Sunday after Thanksgiving. While you're in town, visit Wheeler House, the historic home maintained by the society, and don't miss the Bradley-Wheeler Barn, a unique Connecticut landmark located behind Wheeler House. The seven-sided native cobblestone building with an octagonal roof is believed to be the only one like it in the state. The 1850 barn has been restored and houses a museum that tells the history of Westport.

The Holiday House Tour in Granby, usually held early in December, takes in six houses in and around Granby, both new and old. The homes are holiday decorated and feature live music. You can also tour the historical society's eighteenth-century Weed/Enders House and the Abijah Rowe house—the oldest remnant of Salmon Brook, the British settlement founded in 1680 that would eventually become Granby. Dishes from the historical society's own cookbook are served by members.

Christmas Past

You can step back in time every other Christmas season in Milford. That's when the Milford Historical Society chooses a brand-new theme for its holiday tour of the society's antique homes.

One year, for instance, you could have walked into the pages of your favorite Christmas stories in its Storybook Christmas candlelight tour, held at the Eels-Stowe House. Built in 1700 and believed to be the oldest house in Milford, the Eels-Stowe House is part of the Wharf Lane historic complex, named for the old street that ran from the town dock to the green.

For Storybook Christmas, the Eels-Stowe parlor is laid out as it might have been for Meg, Amy, and Jo's holiday in the classic tale by Louisa May Alcott, *Little Women.* The kitchen is decorated according to a passage from Laura Ingalls Wilder's *Little House in the Big Woods,* says historical society member Pam Hudak. Society members re-created gifts given by the characters in the book: A carved wooden shelf that Pa made for Ma hangs on the wall, while on the table, wrapped in paper and twine, are the mittens that Ma knitted for Pa.

Swedish celebrations are found around the state. This Santa Lucia pageant was presented by the young people at Emanuel Lutheran Church in Hartford.

The bedroom is all ready for a little girl to open her eyes on Christmas morning, if that little girl stepped out of *The Little Princess* by Frances Hodgson Burnett. It's filled with porcelain-faced dolls and fine clothes that could have been purchased from the finest stores.

Another year the theme was Immigrant Christmas—an exploration of the rich ethnic traditions incorporated into local residents' Christmas celebrations.

Inside the Eels-Stowe House, Barbara Vilchinskus Schmidt lays a Lithuanian table for Christmas Eve. At a typical dinner a dozen dishes are served, representing the twelve apostles. Barbara is dressed in a native costume and bedecked in jewelry made of amber, known as Lithuanian gold. "It's petrified resin, which came from ancient trees that grew in the Baltic area," she explains as she fingers the large yellow beads of the necklace.

In a room dedicated to the Polish families in town, there are red and green Christmas wafers to be broken apart and shared by dinner guests. Straw is spread beneath the linen tablecloth to represent the manger where Christ was born.

Another room is dedicated to the Swedish celebration of the feast of Santa Lucia on December 13, which marks the beginning of the Christmas season. In some families the oldest daughter dresses as the saint, wearing a white gown and a wreath of evergreens on her head. The wreath is studded with candles, because Santa Lucia is known as the patron saint of light. According to Pam Hudak, the young Christian woman was martyred in the fourth century in Sicily after giving away her wedding dowry to the poor. "Swedes have a special devotion to the saint," Pam says. A traditional way to mark her day is for the "Lucia maiden" to carry steaming coffee and *lussekatter,* or saffron-flavored buns, to her family for breakfast.

The Nathan Clark Stockade House was the first house built outside the stockade that protected the earliest residents of Milford from the Indians. It was constructed in 1659, and rebuilt in 1780. Inside, Mike Petrucelli is setting the table for an Italian feast. "Christmas is basically a get-together for family," he says. "That's what it's all about. That and food!"

In a room devoted to the Irish, a candle lights the way for Mary and Joseph on their journey to Bethlehem. And if we're all a little bit Irish on St. Patrick's Day, then we must be a bit German on Christmas, too, because so many of our American traditions—like the decorated tree—come from Germany. The front parlor's tree is decorated lavishly with glass ornaments from Munich.

"Christmastime, we always had a stocking at the bottom of the bed," Isabelle Voytek says, remembering childhood in her native Scotland. As she lays out kilts and needlework on a table in the bedroom, she continues, "In Scotland in those days we didn't celebrate a big Christmas. It was a holy day for church." Christmas was declared a holiday in Scotland only in the 1960s.

The third house in the historic Wharf's Lane complex contains a gift shop stocked with Christmas gifts, holiday items, and ethnic goodies. The Milford Historical Society's holiday tour takes place in early December in even-numbered years. You can see the homes by daylight or candlelight.

The Pleasure of Your Company

With its magnificent collection of paintings by Monet, Manet, and Degas, the Farmington home known as Hill-Stead hardly needs ornamentation at the holidays. But its designer and owner, Theodate Pope Riddle, loved to entertain, and at Christmas her gracious home was the scene of elegant gatherings.

A pioneer woman architect, Theodate designed the thirty-nine-room mansion, now a National Historic Landmark, in 1901 for her parents, Alfred and Ada Pope. When they passed away, Theodate moved in with her husband, John Wallace Riddle, a career diplomat. Hill-Stead continued to be a vibrant social center, as it had been when Alfred and Ada were living.

"They had guests from all over the world," says present-day curator Cynthia Cormier. "Well-known authors, politicians, and artists flocked here."

The great novelist Henry James once called Hill-Stead "an exquisite palace of peace, light, and harmony." Sinclair Lewis, Thornton Wilder, Mary Cassatt, and Eleanor Roosevelt were among the guests, and you can be, too. Early in December the staff re-creates the holidays at Hill-Stead, dressing in costume and portraying members of the Pope and Riddle families as they ready for an evening of entertaining.

Curator Cynthia Cormier says visitors enjoy "a glimpse of life as it was actually lived by the Pope and Riddle families in the winter season."

In her bedroom, Theodate's sparkly frock is laid out on her bed, waiting for the lady of the house to slip into it. In Mr. Riddle's room, an antique Santa costume is spread on the chaise, in case Mr. Riddle should choose to portray Saint Nick for his guests.

The butler greets you in the library, where a Whistler scene called *Blue Wave* hangs over the fireplace and an ocean of white poinsettias is banked before the mantel. Theodate believed there should be no division between the commanding views outdoors and the home's interiors, so her holiday decorations were inspired by the natural environment, with pine garlands on the staircase and ivy laced through crystal chandeliers, wreaths hung from window frames and berries and boughs adorning a writing desk.

The dining room is set for a Christmas feast with silver serving pieces from Tiffany & Co. gleaming on the table, alongside the Lenox china with its star-patterned border. The multicourse menu begins with oysters and includes quail with truffles and a Nesselrode pudding.

Outside the house, wreaths decorate doorways, and a dusting of snow highlights Theodate's sunken garden.

Theodate married John Riddle rather late in life, and they never had any children of their own. But she did take in three young boys to raise, although she never formally adopted them. In the drawing room a Christmas tree appears to be waiting for them, with toys and games like tiddlywinks spread beneath its branches.

When Theodate Pope Riddle died in 1946, she left Hill-Stead as a museum, with its impressionist art collection, Chinese porcelains, original furnishings, and gardens intact. According to her instructions, it is maintained today almost precisely the way it was when Theodate lived here.

More Historical Holidays in Farmington

Meet the Family: Holiday at Hill-Stead is only one of the ways to celebrate the season in Farmington. The town's Holiday in the Village celebration also includes a chance to step back farther in time and experience the holidays in one of Farmington's earliest homes, the Stanley-Whitman House. Enjoy a tour of the house with costumed guides, and pretend you are visiting on a winter day in the 1700s. New England artisans sell crafts, and hearty Colonial soups and breads are served for lunch. In the evening some of Farmington's best chefs offer hors d'oeuvres and a wine tasting.

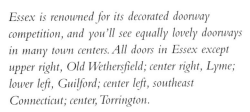

Essex is renowned for its decorated doorway competition, and you'll see equally lovely doorways in many town centers. All doors in Essex except upper right, Old Wethersfield; center right, Lyme; lower left, Guilford; center left, southeast Connecticut; center, Torrington.

Christmas with the First Family

First Lady Claudia Weicker started a tradition that was embraced by First Lady Patty Rowland, inviting the people of Connecticut to visit the governor's home at the holidays. And that means that on the Sunday after Thanksgiving, Patty Rowland is supervising a volunteer team of twenty-five florists, decking the halls of the mansion. But they use more than boughs of holly. When they're finished, the residence is a sparkling showcase of Christmas trees and poinsettias grown in Connecticut.

Since moving in, Mrs. Rowland has overseen the $1.5 million refurbishing of the residence that began during the Weickers' stay here. The house had been neglected: the night that plaster fell onto visiting dignitaries in the dining room, Mrs. Weicker found new support for the renovation campaign, which has been paid for with contributions from corporations and private individuals. The Governor's Residence Conservancy, a private not-for-profit organization established in 1991, is now responsible for preservation of the stately home.

In the Wedgwood blue foyer, five varieties of Connecticut-grown poinsettias in shades of pink, peach, and ivory bank the grand staircase. In the front parlor, the parquetry floor incorporates the state seal with its Latin motto, *Sustinet qui transtulit* (he who transplants sustains). Patty Rowland reveals, "We put a time capsule underneath in case this house ever comes down. They will know what life was like here."

Mrs. Rowland is partial to Victorian themes in design and decorating, so the parlor's holiday tree is wrapped in shimmery mauve French ribbon and hung with golden cherubs, blossoms of dried hydrangea, and frosted fruits. On the sideboard in the formal dining room, a magnificent silver tea service gleams.

"This is the silver service that was made in 1909 by International Silver in Meriden to commemorate the USS *Connecticut,*" says the first lady. "It's been at the state library. It used to be here at the residence, and so we've brought it back." Scenes on the silver pieces depict naval battles, ships of Connecticut, and the Capitol in Hartford. It seems to belong here, among other pieces of art and antiques on loan from some of the state's museums.

The dining room is elegant, with wall coverings of silk damask and dried amaranthus hanging from the fireplace mantel like cranberry-colored icicles. The seat cushions of the Chippendale-style chairs have been stitched by the Connecticut Valley Embroiderer's Guild.

One year Christopher Radko decorated the living room tree, with glass ornaments made in

Eastern Europe. In other years the tree has featured Victorian-style paper ornaments crafted by Connecticut artist Patti Kierys. Her designs featured some of Connecticut's famous faces, from the governor to Paul Newman, Mark Twain, and Rebecca Lobo. (Read more about the ornaments on page 81.)

The sunroom, warmed by yellow paint and wicker furniture, is scented by an elaborate gingerbread village. "They represent historic buildings all over the state," Mrs. Rowland explains, pointing to the carousel at Lighthouse Point Park in New Haven, the Goodspeed Opera House in Haddam, and the Soldiers and Sailors Arch in Bushnell Park. The gingerbread will be auctioned off for charity.

The first family's children decorate the sunroom tree with their own ornaments. Giant Lego toys, designed by the artists at their factory in Enfield, stand guard beneath the balsam. In the library, where wooden cabinets have recently been installed, stands the tree the governor chopped down himself, decorated with the first lady's

own ornaments, lovingly collected over the years. One of them is her mother's baby rattle.

Since the Rowlands took up residence in 1994, Mrs. Rowland has stamped her own style on the holidays here, starting with the governor's official holiday card. She called on a friend from Woodbury for its design, which features the governor's residence aglow on a winter's evening. "We tried to capture the residence on Christmas Eve, with my sons' room lit. We're in the library, trying to put the tree together."

The card's design has been cast in brass as a Christmas tree ornament. The annual collectible ornaments are for sale during the holiday home tour. The proceeds help pay for the continuing care of the mansion.

The Rowlands are the twelfth family to live in the governor's official residence, which was purchased in 1943. The three-story brick and limestone Georgian revival–style home has nineteen rooms, nine fireplaces, a greenhouse, a pergola, and a reflecting pool set on six acres at 990 Prospect Avenue, at the corner of Asylum Avenue.

If you'd like to visit, the annual Holiday Open House Tour begins the Wednesday after Thanksgiving. Admission is one new unwrapped toy to be given to a needy child. On the first morning of the open house, the governor and first lady are often there to welcome the people of Connecticut to their home.

Barns get the holiday touch, clockwise from upper left: Chester, Guilford, South Windsor, Newtown, Woodbridge, Weston, Sandy Hook, North Stamford, Chester.

Heart and Hand

Every morning as I dress for work, I check the top of my antique pine bureau. Memos to myself, shopping lists, or mail to send is gathered beneath a fist-sized beach stone, smoothed by waves and the sand, and oil painted with an old-time whaling scene by John Wilson of Westbrook. I lift a pair of hand-hammered earrings out of a walnut jewelry box, planed and buffed to a satiny sheen by a local woodworker. The jewelry box was a Christmas gift, purchased at the Creative Arts Workshop when we lived just across the street in New Haven. Adjusting the earrings, I glance in the mirror, framed by hand-hewn cherry wood and inset with hand-glazed tiles. The mirror was an engagement gift from my sister Debb, and her image appears momentarily in the glass each time I glance into it. In the kitchen I grab a tea bag from the canister Debb decorated as a housewarming gift for my very first apartment, the one I moved into the week after my college graduation. I pour boiling water into a favorite mug. I watched the potter throw it on a wheel and sign it before she stacked it carefully in the kiln at the Guilford Handcraft Center. Finishing the tea, I place the cup on a mat loomed in Litchfield, and carry them to the counter on a decoupage tray made by my sister Suki. Before walking out the front door, I snap off the lamp, the one with the image of Cornwall Bridge glazed on its willowware base.

Gifts from the heart? You bet, and because heart and hand go hand in hand, my most treasured gifts are the ones that are handmade. At Christmas we seem even more compelled to share a bit of our hearts. Handmade gifts range from the simple to the simply wonderful. Who hasn't been thrilled to receive a still-warm pumpkin loaf fresh from the oven of a dear friend or neighbor? Better yet, how about delivering a basket brimming over with the providence of Connecticut?

And if you've no time or inclination to make your own holiday presents, consider shopping at one of the state's crafts centers or a unique department store for a one-of-a-kind keepsake that bears the fingerprints of a Connecticut artisan. In nearly every city, town, and village in our state there are artists, cooks, craftspeople, and small businesses turning out products that are handmade and homegrown; that reflect Yankee ingenuity and Connecticut creativity. Sharing the bounty that is *made in Connecticut*—it's even more special at this time of year.

Left: Katharine Hepburn as a Victorian bicyclist and, above right, a cornucopia, both by Patti Kierys.

Christmas in the Mansion

If you need to get in the mood for shopping, an array of holiday fund-raising boutiques across the state may fit the bill. Perhaps the most spectacular is Christmas in the Mansion, a showcase of the season at the Academy of Our Lady of Mercy, Lauralton Hall in Milford. Lauralton Hall is the oldest Catholic girls' college preparatory school in Connecticut, founded in 1905, and the holiday showcase is the school's largest fund-raiser. The magnificent mansion is a Victorian Gothic gem that dates to the Civil War era. Charles Hobby Pond, who would go on to be Connecticut's governor, built the home in 1864. He christened it Island View because its tower offered an unobstructed view of Charles Island and Long Island Sound. Henry August Taylor bought the house in 1889 and renamed it Lauralton Hall after his deceased mother and daughter, both named Laura. Taylor remodeled the mansion, adding a round tower, a veranda, and the mahogany staircase that dominates the lovely entryway. In 1905 Taylor sold the estate to the Sisters of Mercy for thirty-five-thousand dollars and asked that it always be called Lauralton Hall. Some students claim to have seen the ghost of young Laura wandering through her family's former home.

The grandeur of the mansion lives on, with classrooms graced by fireplaces with elaborately carved mantels inset with imported Dutch tiles. The chapel, up a grand staircase, is pristinely breathtaking. During Thanksgiving weekend each year, a committee of volunteers decorates Lauralton Hall extravagantly with thousands of ornaments, hundreds of feet of garland, five hundred bows, and more than two

thousand feet of ribbon. In the boardroom florist Edward Dillon creates memorable mantelpiece displays—like the snowman he once crafted from hundreds of white football mums and barely blushing roses.

Three floors in the mansion and classroom wing are transformed into boutiques, and the dining hall and auditorium accommodate more than fifty vendors selling home furnishings, holiday gifts, decorations, ornaments, fine arts and crafts, jewelry, vintage clothing, gourmet food items, and delicious baked goods. Hundreds of white luminaria light the quarter-mile-long driveway leading to the mansion on the first evening of the three-day event, generally held the first weekend in December. Fifteen thousand visitors ooh and ahh over the decorations and the architecture, enjoying periodic concerts throughout the weekend by the high school glee club. Looking for an impressive place for your holiday party? The mansion is available for rent once the holiday showcase is over.

Noel Boutique

Another way to make your holiday spending count is to visit the annual Noel Boutique sponsored by the New Britain Junior League. The event is the premier annual fund-raiser for the Junior League and in twenty years has raised more than half a million dollars for community projects, such as the Diagnostic Breast Center at New Britain General Hospital and the revitalization of the New Britain Youth Museum. The three-day event in the parish hall at St. Maurice's features about two dozen specialty retail stores or boutiques from throughout the Northeast. It runs from the first Thursday through the first Saturday of November.

Made in Connecticut

For better than 110 years, Howland Hughes Department Store has been a landmark in downtown Waterbury. Hank Paine's family has owned the store for three generations. "It's been a way of life, and folks who have worked here have become lifelong friends forever," he says.

But in the early 1990s, that way of life was fading for Hank and his loyal shoppers. With an influx of national chain stores at the malls, Howland Hughes was having a hard time competing. "We weren't on a level playing field," Hank says. "We needed to do something different."

"Something different" meant reinventing Howland Hughes as a store that sells only merchandise made in Connecticut, anything from flags to furniture. "We're showing something that none of the malls, none of the big stores has the opportunity to show," Hank says proudly, "and that's the incredible ingenuity, value, and quality of 'made in Connecticut.'"

There are replicas of state monuments and lighthouses made to sit on your shelf, and handcrafted copper weather vanes for your rooftop. Woodbury pewter gleams from inside a glass display case. Onaments carved from the trunks of Christmas trees are made nearby.

The store carries brass buttons, made for more than two centuries by Waterbury Companies Inc., which has supplied the military, sports tournaments, and clothing makers, as well as the crew of the *Titanic*. Each silk necktie from Allyn Neckwear in Stamford has a name, like Ex-Libris. Bovano in Cheshire makes glass enamel sculptures, and warm woolen blankets are woven by Chas. W. House and Sons in Unionville. Shelves are lined with scented candles made by Liberty Candle in Bolton. There's weedash and cathedral glass from Plumb Hill Studios in Washington, and collectible dolls sculpted in Litchfield. Chimes ring out from a wall filled with elegant precision clocks made in Farmington.

With his homespun philosophy and deep belief in old-fashioned values, Hank doesn't come off much like a slick salesman. Maybe that's because he's also a Vermont farmer.

He chuckles softly and shakes his head as he says, "I'm probably a better farmer than I am a retailer, but my neighbors on the farm say I am probably a better retailer than I am a farmer."

How many retailers do you know who like to quote Mark Twain's *A Connecticut Yankee in King Arthur's Court*? For Hank it has become something of a creed. "In the first page of that book the hero identifies himself. He says, 'I'm an American. I was born in Hartford in the great state of Connecticut. I was trained in the great factories there. We can make anything, anything in the world, anything a body wanted. If I couldn't make a thing, I invented it.'"

And Hank Paine hopes to show this state that the people here can still do that. For holiday gifts made in Connecticut, head for Howland Hughes, the Connecticut store.

Goodies from Home

Jams, salsas, maple syrup, honey, vinegars, oils, mustards, candy, sauces, and marinated mushrooms are just a few of the culinary delights that you'll find at Connecticut Creative, the store located at the Department of Agriculture.

Only products made in Connecticut are sold here, and you may be surprised by the array of gourmet goodies—ranging from Linda Shallah's Savory Fare dried bean soup mixes to maple-sugar-coated pecans from Rob Lamothe's Burlington Sugar House. The store features nearly one hundred products made by forty-eight small companies.

Among my favorites are the raspberry jams from Rose's Berry Farm in South Glastonbury. There is so much fruit in the jam, and it's so lightly sweetened, that it's almost like eating the berries right from the bushes in the warmth of a sunny July day. Thinking of hot mulled cider or wassail for your holiday gathering? You'll want the mulling spices from Sundial Gardens in Higganum. There are many ways to enliven your holiday table with Snydi Idi's Nip 'N Tang fruited horseradish sauce made in South Windsor.

Selected crafts from Connecticut artisans are also sold in the store, along with "Connecticut Grown" and UConn apparel and novelty items. Gift baskets chock-full of Connecticut-made goodies and treats can be ordered for Christmas gifts, or for any occasion, and shipped anywhere in the continental United States. Choose one already made or customize a basket with your own selections. To help you decide what to include, think about shopping on the day of the open house and tasting at the start of the holiday season. You'll also have a chance to meet some of the food purveyors.

Handmade Holiday

If you're looking for a one-of-a-kind gift, head to the one of five nonprofit centers located along the Trail of Connecticut Crafts Centers. In November and December the creations of more than a thousand American craftsartists are displayed here at holiday exhibitions and sales. Proceeds support the centers, which offer a wide range of classes and workshops in the visual arts.

The *Guilford Handcraft Center* is located in a converted mill. The holiday sale of fine crafts and art features more than three hundred invited and juried artists from across the nation, including dozens from Connecticut. Museum-quality ceramics, glass, basketry, quilts, and more are featured. The sale benefits the center, providing scholarships and helping the center maintain its studios and gallery to present the work of local artists, such as Anita Griffith and Robert Parrot of Madison. Anita and Robert collaborate in life and in their work. The husband and wife turn out every piece of pottery together: Robert throws them on the wheel, while Anita decorates them. Their Spanish-style majolica pottery is popular among shoreline collectors.

The holiday sale showcases the latest trends in American crafts. Executive Director Jennifer Aniskovich says of gift buying here: "It's a chance for those who are inspired by the arts to share a sliver of beauty with a loved one." On Nonprofit Shopping Day, five percent of each sale is donated to a nonprofit organization specified by the shopper.

Founded in 1957, the Guilford Handcraft Center nurtures more than three thousand five hundred students a year, who study everything from basketry and beading to blacksmithing, pottery, sculpture, and weaving. The shop is open seven days a week, and the sale generally begins early in November and lasts through Christmas Eve.

From Guilford, travel north to Middletown to *Wesleyan Potters*, located in the heart of the Connecticut River Valley. The center is named for its first location on the campus of Wesleyan University, where in 1948 a professor taught pottery making to local residents. The center now occupies a former venetian blind factory. These days you'll find more than just pottery here. The center and school are run by a cooperative guild of craftsartists who specialize in metal, clay, and fiber. During the annual holiday sale, more than two hundred artists are featured; items range from objets d'art to children's toys. Cafe nights feature music and light refreshments while you shop.

If you drive northwest to Avon, you'll find the *Farmington Valley Arts Center* located in a quiet, wooded, parklike setting not far from area shops and dining spots. The center was founded in the 1970s in refurbished brownstone buildings once occupied by a safety fuse manufacturer. The educational center is now home to more than forty

Previous page: One-of-a-kind crafts from the Guilford Handcraft Center. This page, clockwise from top left: Hilles Gallery at the Creative Arts Workshop; a view of Wesleyan Potters' annual exhibition and sale; wooden puzzle and carved gourd vessels, all from Creative Arts Workshop.

resident studio artists. The shop sells contemporary American crafts and art. A recent renovation project enlarged the gallery's display area.

The *Brookfield Craft Center* celebrated the twenty-fifth anniversary of its Holiday Exhibition and Sale recently with a new twist: It offered shoppers the chance to create unique gifts of their own. Four entry-level workshops were offered in printmaking, folded paper gift boxes, tinsmithed ornaments, and everlasting wreaths. The center is located along the Still River in a historic gristmill that dates to 1780. The work of over two hundred artists is on display at the Holiday Exhibition and Sale. Judith Russell, the curator of the show, says, "You can exercise creativity just in the gifts you select."

From Brookfield, travel southeast to the heart of New Haven's Audubon Arts District, where the *Creative Arts Workshop* displays the work of more than 450 artists in a dramatic two-story windowed gallery. The workshop is located within walking distance of Yale University and New Haven's historic green in an area populated by galleries, restaurants, and coffeehouses. Artists from all over the United States, with a special emphasis on Connecticut, are featured in the annual Celebration of American Crafts. The choices are eclectic and exciting, with jewelry, clothing, furniture, and housewares on the

cutting edge of the contemporary crafts movement. This is a great place to find a museum-quality end table, an unusual pin or pair of earrings, a wonderful evening bag, or even a patchwork pillow made from antique Japanese kimonos.

Paper Dolls

At one home in New Hartford, it's Christmas all year long.

"I love the holidays. They've always been very special to me," says Patti Kierys, who stitches and glues for months, creating ornaments for not one but several holiday trees, and some pretty impressive ones at that. Besides her own trees, Patti has made ornaments for trees at the Smithsonian, the governor's residence, and the Pageant of Peace in Washington, D.C.; that tree, representing Connecticut, stands outside the White House.

Patti is especially careful in crafting the Victorian-style ornaments for the tree that stands in the entryway to the Smithsonian Institution. "Being that it's the national museum of American history," she says, "it has to be authentic to that period."

Patti has decorated that tree three times. On the first occasion she spent nine months making ornaments, and even that wasn't enough. She recalls, "It was so huge that even my 450 ornaments looked a little dwarfed on it, so I took everything that I had planned to put under the tree and I was hanging it *on* the tree!"

Patti is a nationally known expert on Victorian ornaments, which she reproduces using crepe paper, cotton batting, and chromolithographs just like the ones women collected in scrapbooks in the 1800s. Birch bark collected on a walk in the woods forms a cornucopia, and a tiny baby doll is wrapped in fabric from the sleeve of a dress that once belonged to Patti's daughter.

For several years Connecticut's first ladies asked Patti to decorate a special tree in the governor's residence. Patti crafted Connecticut personalities, ranging from Rebecca Lobo to Paul Newman to Harriet Beecher Stowe, all decked out for a Victorian ball.

Some of the ornaments made a gentle political statement. "When I did Governor Weicker, I dressed him up in dollar-sign pants. He represented the income tax period, and it was my subtle way of sliding that in," she chuckles.

When First Lady Patty Rowland suggested the tree's theme be tourism, Patti created miniatures of state landmarks, including Mark Twain's house and the arch at Bushnell Park. Recently Patti has branched out, making more ornaments that represent angels. Some are Victorian in style, others are designed with faces made from clay, and some are molded from beeswax. They are for sale at the Healing Hearts Center in Canton, where her daughter practices Reiki and natural healing.

Although she works almost around the clock making her holiday ornaments, Patti keeps Christmas in her heart. "I never want to lose that sparkle of enthusiasm over a special holiday," she says fervently. And she makes the holidays sparkle for the rest of us.

Left: Fans, angels, and popcorn garlands on a tree at the Mark Twain House.

Gifts from the Sea

When travelers from as far away as China stop at the Silver Skate Christmas Shop in Niantic, Pat Lewis steers them to a case filled with hand-painted shell ornaments. "As far as any ornament goes from New England, this one is the best," says Pat. "It's a true souvenir of Connecticut."

The ornaments are created by John Wilson in a grand old weathered house on the shore of the Menunketesuck River in Westbrook. John is standing on the riverbank feeding the ducks. "We moved here from Meriden in 1941 and I've always liked the water," he says, tossing crusts from a loaf of bread to the quacking mallards.

John worked for International Silver in Meriden, but when the company folded, he decided

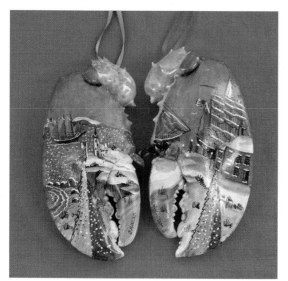

to try his luck working from home, using artistic skills that had been dormant since his high school days. With pen and ink, John turns beach stones, polished by the surf, into paperweights.

"I sold them by the ton," he laughs. "It's enjoyable, too, because I love the beach anyway. I'd gather the stones in the wintertime because they seem to disappear in the summertime. I go clamming and just enjoy the day and pick up some stones for drawing."

Soon John started drawing and painting his nautical scenes on steamer and scallop shells, sand dollars, and even lobster claws—all of which, he discovered, make great Christmas tree ornaments. Painting on unusual objects is something of a family tradition. In his dining room, John points to a treasured set of dessert dishes decorated with delicate pink dogwood blossoms. "My grandfather Walter Wilson is well known in Connecticut, especially in the Meriden and New Haven areas, for hand-decorating china. Of course, he is no longer with us, and his work is available now only through private collectors and in some antiques shops."

John paints scenes of lighthouses, harbors, and old-time whaling ships. "I don't do any modern drawing," he says. "It's all from the days of sail. That's all I am interested in. I don't like powerboats, which I call 'stinkpots.' I love sailboats."

John's love of sail and sea is apparent in his home and its maritime decor, adorned with ship's models and ship's wheels and a collection of antique Nantucket scrimshaw. His hand-painted shells dangle from a pewter chandelier over the dining room table. It's the perfect setting for an artist to re-create scenes from long ago, scenes on shells that bring a touch of Connecticut to so many Christmas trees.

Crafted in Connecticut, clockwise from top right: one of Susan Miller-Ceskavich's Jingle Balls; Diana Mihaltse's tin folk-art Santa; wreath from the Mashantucket Pequot Tribal Nation tree; wooden ornament by Primrose Path; Joan Hepburn's hand-blown glass ornaments.

A Living Doll House

They say a man's home is his castle, but some homes are more like castles than others. With its towers and turrets, fieldstone walls, and commanding views, designer Louis Nichole's home in a Waterbury suburb is the Connecticut equivalent.

"Since I was a little kid, I always said that I was gonna live in a castle. My relatives always said, 'Oh yeah, little Louie says he's gonna live in a castle.' When I bought this, it was so funny," Louis says, smiling as he remembers. "They all came up and said, 'I can't believe you bought this house.' It's always been my dream since I was a little kid."

Beyond spectacular—Louis Nichole's Emma doll and (right) his dining room set for holiday festivities.

Louis's dream house started out as a country club. "It had a pro shop, four dining rooms, four kitchens, and a banquet hall. It has a golf course, and it had parking for one thousand people. To me it was like an empty canvas. I didn't see it for what it was, but what it could be."

And what it could be, Louis thought, was a palace. But he needed his family's help to make it one. "My 235 Italian relatives from Waterbury spent about six months completely gutting wall after wall after wall," he says. Then they installed paneled rooms salvaged from an eighteenth-century palace in Europe.

"I grew up in Waterbury on Englewood Avenue . . . hello! We lived in a three-family house. I never knew those kinds of things existed," he says of the exquisite paneling. But he distinctly recalls the first time he saw it on the auction block. "I walked into the room and my heart started pounding. I can't explain the feeling but it felt like I was connected to this paneling from some other century." So he bought it.

Louis furnished his elegant home with some antiques, but mostly with furniture, wallpaper, and fabrics that he designed himself. "This is the house that reject built. Almost everything in here is something of my line in the early 1980s that didn't sell," he says with a smile.

So how does an ex–kindergarten teacher turned designer end up living in a place like this? You might say it was another house that bought Louis this house—the White House. After a 1979 magazine story on the struggling young designer, Louis got a phone call.

"I'll never forget it. She said, 'Hello, Louis, this is Rosalynn Carter from the White House.' And I said, 'Auntie Margie'—I thought it was my Aunt Margie, who does voices—'that is the

worst imitation of Rosalynn Carter I've ever heard in my life.' And there was dead silence. It was about two minutes later when I realized it wasn't a joke." He laughs. "Mrs. Carter had seen my work in *Good Housekeeping*."

The first lady invited Louis to decorate the White House, from table linens to Christmas trees. "When you have a thirty-foot tree, you can't put tiny ornaments on it. So I said to myself, *Let me make three-foot dolls to hang on it.*"

The dolls were a hit, and a new business was launched. Today Louis Nichole is known for his line of lovely dolls and for his Christmas ornaments. "When people see this kind of quality, and it's still made today, it makes our ornaments quite collectible."

Recently Louis donated two thousand copies of the White House dolls to Waterbury's Mattatuck Museum for its annual fund-raiser known as the Festival of the Trees.

"The idea was to send the dolls out into the community, to have people dress them in their kitchens, in their classrooms, in their schools, and in elderly housing," says Marie Galbraith, the Mattatuck's executive director. "Then we brought all of the dolls back and put them on display with the Christmas trees in the museum galleries. Louis has given the museum the opportunity to reach out to the community and the community an opportunity to express its creativity by creating these doll costumes." Some of the costumed dolls are sold, raising more than ten thousand dollars annually for the museum.

"To me Christmas is about family and exchanging a part of yourself," says Louis. And Louis Nichole has given a part of himself to the Mattatuck Museum. Whether it's donating dolls to the tree festival or offering his home for gala museum fund-raisers, he's designing a Connecticut Christmas celebration that captures the holiday's true meaning.

Mattatuck Festival of the Trees

The Mattatuck Museum's Festival of the Trees has ushered in the holiday season in Waterbury for ten years. The ten-day festival showcases hundreds of dolls and trees for sale, decorated and donated by area residents, groups, schools, and businesses. One crowd-pleaser is the twelve-foot-tall Brass City Express featuring seven trains traveling around the tree. Storytellers, magicians, puppeteers, bell ringers, dancers, and choral groups perform throughout the festival, which begins right after Thanksgiving.

Holiday trees in all shapes and sizes, clockwise from top right: Wadsworth Atheneum trees in Hartford, the tree on the New Haven town green, two views of homey decor, glitter at the Pink Sleigh in Westbrook, and an impressionistic tree at the Florence Griswold Museum in Old Lyme (center).

Santa's Architect

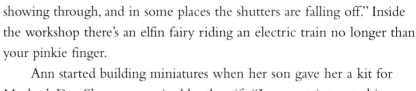

In Ann Hughes's home it's Christmas all year long. "I'd love to see Christmas around 365 days a year," she says. "To me it brings a tremendous amount of joy and happiness."

Santa, his elves, and sugarplum fairies populate Ann's homes; she's even been dubbed Santa's Architect. But in Ann's world, Santa's workshop is less than three feet tall, and the jolly old elf himself stands only several inches high. Ann's houses are miniatures, and each one tells a story.

"I try to make them look like they've been around a while," Ann explains. "There's bricks

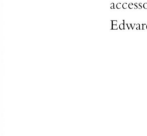

showing through, and in some places the shutters are falling off." Inside the workshop there's an elfin fairy riding an electric train no longer than your pinkie finger.

Ann started building miniatures when her son gave her a kit for Mother's Day. She was surprised by the gift. "I was not interested in miniatures; I knew nothing about miniatures. But I felt guilty when I didn't put it together, so I finally put it together, and I was hooked."

After building that first simple house, Ann started construction of a tabletop Edwardian mansion, but stopped to design and build a new house for her real family. Ann is trained in architectural engineering, which helps her design these intricate tiny Santa homes, like the lighthouse where Santa and Mrs. Claus go on vacation. Even at his vacation place, Santa is well furnished and outfitted—down to L.L. Bean boots the size of your thumbnail.

The dollhouse furniture you might have played with as a child would seem large compared to the furniture in Ann's little homes. As more adults have taken up collecting miniatures, the furniture has shrunk, and it's precisely tiny. Mrs. Claus sits in a rocking chair based on a real one, but scaled down perfectly, so that one foot becomes one inch, or even one-half or one-quarter inch.

Ann's miniatures have taken top prizes at the New England and Philadelphia Flower Shows. She's even taken on commissioned work, including a miniature version of one of Fairfield's loveliest Victorian homes. It was a gift to the owner for her fortieth birthday.

Ann concentrates on building the homes and furniture. She collects the characters and accessories from "mini" makers all over the world. That's how she created Christmas Eve in her Edwardian mansion. Ann's brother wrote the poem that brings the scene to life:

> 'Tis the night before Christmas in this Edwardian house,
> not a creature is stirring, 'cept maybe a mouse,
> and the toddler who's sitting up there on the stair,
> with Teddy and blankie, his cuddling pair.
> The stockings are hung by the chimney with care.
> Mama dog with her pups by the stove is so warm,
> the whole house is cozy, who cares if it storms,
> this old-fashioned Christmas is a wonderful sight,
> Merry Christmas to all, and to all a good night.

Santa's jolly presence is felt throughout the state, clockwise from top left: Old Saybrook, Madison, Bridgeport, Guilford, Lyme, Norwalk, Mystic, and Old Saybrook (center).

Visions of Sugarplums

When I was a child growing up in New York, the magic of the holiday season began on Thanksgiving. My sisters and brother and cousins took the subway with our dads into Manhattan for the Macy's parade. My grandfather's office was on the parade route, at eye level with the huge balloons that are its trademark. When the parade was over, we all squeezed into my grandparents' apartment for a turkey dinner. As a special treat, my sister and one of my cousins and I slept over

on a pullout couch in the living room. The next day my grandmother took us to Radio City Music Hall for the Christmas show with the Rockettes and the opening of the season's big Disney movie. The lines wrapped around the building, and we held each other's hands tight so we wouldn't get separated.

After my grandfather retired, we lost our special vantage point over the parade, and our holiday traditions changed. The day after Thanksgiving was when we sat down with pencils and lined paper and—in our best penmanship—wrote our letters to Santa. They were wish lists of all the toys we hoped he

would bring, promising that we had been very good children. We left them in our stockings on December 6, Saint Nicholas's feast day, for delivery to the North Pole.

During our holiday vacation from school, my mom would take us to see the wonderful windows of the major department stores—Saks Fifth Avenue, Best and Company, Lord and Taylor, and B. Altman's—decorated with animated figures and fantasy themes. For several years Mom and Dad's offices overlooked Rockefeller Center, and they'd hold their company party the evening of the tree lighting. High above the crowds, we pressed our noses to the windows to see the tree's lights come on.

Years later I felt that same childlike thrill when, as a television news anchor, I was sent to cover the arrival of Santa in downtown New Haven. Other reporters balked at covering what they considered a "puff piece," preferring to work on the hard news stories they thought of as more important. But as I stood before the cameras reporting live, surrounded and jostled by excited and squealing kids, I felt the joy of the season welling up inside. Santa arrived in a fire engine on the New Haven green and was greeted by cheering children. I grinned as Saint Nick led the crowd in a countdown—"5 . . . 4 . . . 3 . . . 2 . . . 1"—and then flipped the switch that lit the giant tree on the green. After that, I made a detour every night as I left the TV station on my way home so that I could drive slowly past the green and its magnificent tree, twinkling with the promise of a Merry Christmas and Happy New Year.

Left: The parlor tree, with antique toys gathered beneath its boughs, at the Hotchkiss-Fyler House Museum, Torrington.

The Santa Special

Model trains have been part of America's Christmas tradition for generations, but you know what they say about men and boys and the size of their toys.

"I just loved trains, and I always wanted to drive a steam engine when I was a boy. Now here I am," says Sepp Markkanen as he climbs into the cab of the vintage locomotive. Sepp's dream came true. He's an engineer on the Valley Railroad's Essex Steam Train. There's still a bit of boyhood wonder in his voice as he says, "It's the largest thing that rolls on the face of the earth. People just love to see the train coming down the tracks."

In December the train to ride is the Santa Special (formerly known as the North Pole Express), powered by a steam engine that goes back to 1925. The steam is generated by coal. Passengers board at the old-fashioned train station, then with a blast from the whistle, the train is on its way. Santa and Mrs. Claus burst into one of the train's antique railroad cars and children shriek with happiness. Little passengers with gleaming eyes whisper their Christmas wishes in Santa's ear.

Eight-year-old Flora Shanker likes Mrs. Claus best, "because she's sweet and I like how she's Santa's wife and how she gets to be with the elves all the time."

Bob and Lisa Teixeira of Mystic are riding the train with their seven-year-old daughter Amy and three-year-old son Luke. "We wanted Luke to experience this while he was young. Little boys seem to have a special liking for trains," says Bob. Lisa adds that riding the Santa Special has become a family tradition. "There's not a lot of hype. We're just here together and we're not spending a lot of money and the kids aren't asking for things at the mall or toys or presents. It's just about being together and riding the train and getting us into the Christmas spirit."

Chester resident Eileen DeWolf is riding the train with friends from Massachusetts. "It's a wonderful way to get together and form special memories of the holiday season. We enjoy it a lot."

Christmas carols play throughout the one-hour trip from Essex to Chester and back. People who live along the tracks have created elaborate displays of lights, making the trips after dusk extra special. Railroad buffs will appreciate the authenticity of the restored parlor cars, but anyone will enjoy leaving today behind and riding off into a winter wonderland in one of the prettiest parts of Connecticut aboard the Essex Steam Train's Santa Special.

The Holiday Express

The Danbury train station was a bustling place when it was built in 1903. If it looks familiar, it may be because it was featured in the Alfred Hitchcock movie *Strangers on a Train*. Today the station has a new life as the Danbury Railway Museum, and it's a holiday favorite for visitors.

"Back in the heyday of railroads there were forty or fifty trains a day that would go through Danbury, freight and passenger and commuter service," says Don Silberbauer. He and his fellow museum volunteers are currently restoring relics of some of the great northeastern train lines. One of the museum's treasures is an open-platform observation car.

"This was at the tail end of the 20th Century Limited," Don explains. "It used to be the premiere New York Central passenger train between New York City and Chicago."

A tour of the railroad yard reveals some oddities, like an experiment tried by the New Haven Railroad in the 1950s as a way to lure passengers back onto the railroads. It was a cross between a bus and a railroad car.

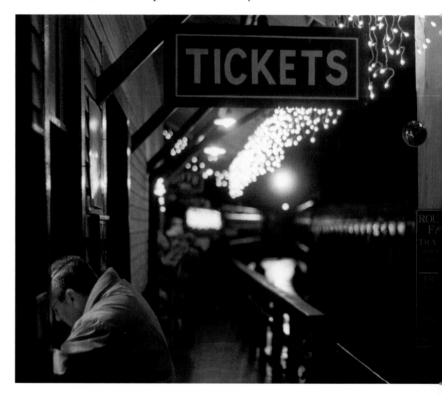

There are also passenger cars from the 1920s and a caboose that was almost a rolling studio apartment. It housed a two-man crew that could stop the train from the caboose if there was trouble, such as dragging equipment, at the rear of the train. "They'd open a valve and let the air out of the brakes and the train would come to an emergency stop," says Don.

Don and his wife, Mickey, spend most of their spare time working on projects at the museum. Mickey hopes a thriving museum will bring tourists into Danbury throughout the year, not

The ticket window at the Valley Railroad in Essex.

just at Christmas. Don hopes to pass along his love of trains to the younger generation. "I was fascinated by trains from the earliest days of my childhood, and I know what it is to bring something with you through the years."

There are special events year-round at the museum, but December features two that are especially popular. An excursion train departs Danbury the first Saturday of the month and heads for New York City. Santa and his helpers are on board. There is also live music, and a rolling brunch is served. Passengers spend several hours in New York shopping and sightseeing, then return to Danbury. Tickets are on sale as early as September, but the excursion always sells out.

The next two weekends in December feature a special event in the train yard. Kids ride a fully decorated train that pulls up alongside a coach where Santa and his elves hold court.

More Holiday Trains and Trolleys

The Railroad Museum of New England, which operates the Naugatuck Railroad, runs scenic Christmas train rides from its historic station in Thomaston to Torrington and Waterville. On weekends right after Thanksgiving through mid-December, vintage cars are decorated for the season and Christmas music plays on board. Santa and Mrs. Claus greet passengers as the train travels through some of the prettiest

countryside in the valley. If it's a white Christmas, the railroad is prepared. It has its own vintage rail snowplow.

Does your gift list include a railroad aficionado? The museum offers what might be the ultimate gift: the chance to be an engineer for an hour. For a fee, licensed drivers over the age of eighteen can test their skills at the controls of a diesel locomotive.

While you're in Thomaston, enjoy the white lights outlining historic buildings like the Thomaston Opera House. The Light Up the Town Celebration on the Saturday after Thanksgiving illuminates the entire downtown.

A three-mile round-trip on an old-fashioned trolley is the featured activity at the *Connecticut Trolley Museum*'s Winterfest, starting just after Thanksgiving and running to the New Year. You'll hear the whistles blow and brass bells ring as antique streetcars take you through the countryside of East Windsor.

The closed cars are finished in mahogany and sport old-fashioned "ad cards." Or you can dress in your warmest winter woolies and brave the chill in a completely open car, which may have Santa as its engineer. At nighttime the trolley takes you through a tunnel of lights, an area decorated just for Christmas.

In East Haven the *Shore Line Trolley Museum* runs the Branford Electric Railway, said to be

the oldest continuously operating suburban trolley line in the United States. On weekends after Thanksgiving the museum offers Santa on the Trolley, complete with cookies, hot chocolate, a Lionel train exhibit, and a take-home gift pack for the kids.

Top left and right: Winterfest at the Connecticut Trolley Museum; below left, the Shore Line Trolley en route.

The Man Who Saved Christmas

Many of us remember a time when it wasn't Christmas until the trains were set up beneath the tree. But for millions of American children, there might never have been any electric trains if not for New Haven toy maker Alfred Carlton Gilbert, who became known as "the man who saved Christmas."

At the Eli Whitney Museum in Hamden, the taped sounds of the heyday of railroading mingle with the excited voices of children, who are clustered around an elaborate model train display. Second-graders are watching model trains made by Gilbert's company circle an exact scale replica of the A. C. Gilbert factory. The huge brick plant, now known as Erector Square, still stands just blocks away from their New Haven school. At one time three thousand people worked there. Although Gilbert is known for his trains and toys, including the Erector Set, toy making was not originally his main business.

"Before the war A. C. Gilbert produced an enormous number of small electrical appliances. The toy business was seasonal. You only produced toys near the holiday times because children didn't get toys any time other than Christmas," says Bill Brown, the curator of the Eli Whitney Museum.

During World War I Gilbert turned his plant over to military production, but he never forgot the kids, even going to Washington to persuade Congress that some production of toys should continue because they were essential to the education and morale of the nation.

"He took his toys along, and the congressmen got down on the floor and put together erector sets," says Bill Brown. "The next day the headline in the *Boston Globe* was 'A. C. Gilbert: The Man Who Saves Christmas.'"

By 1941 A. C. Gilbert was the world's largest toy manufacturer. After the Second World War he began producing model trains, called American Flyers. His company sold steam trains and streamlined trains of the future, representing many of the country's major railroads, most of which are now long gone.

For inspiration, the toy designers could look out the window or walk down the block to the railroad yard, says Bill Brown. "Gilbert had his own railroad siding, and the factory itself was a product of the rail history of New Haven."

The A. C. Gilbert Company is gone now, but Gilbert's model trains are still around, ready for another Christmas. "Gilbert would tell parents, 'These are expensive toys, but trust me, they will last for three generations.' We're running forty-year-old trains in this exhibit—and they're running magnificently," Brown says.

A fitting tribute to the man who saved Christmas.

The train exhibition runs from November through January at the Eli Whitney Museum, with a different layout each year. One backdrop for the trains was an amazing re-creation of New Haven harbor, built by a local theatrical designer and an architect. The museum, which is dedicated to the legacy of inventor Eli Whitney, often incorporates new technology into its train display, including allowing visitors to run trains from its Web site (www.eliwhitney.org).

Right: A quiet winter evening at the train station in Kent.

Bless the beasts at Christmastime, clockwise from upper left: Southington, Clinton, Madison, Fairfield, Westport, Chester.

Christmas Village

Not all dreams come to us while we are sleeping. Carl Bozenski of Torrington dreamed his biggest dreams while he was wide awake, recovering from nearly fatal bouts of tuberculosis. In 1939 Carl became the city's first supervisor of parks and recreation, and the recreational opportunities he created for kids included swimming and track meets in summer and sledding and ice skating in winter. They say Carl worked so hard, and cared so much, that he pushed himself beyond his physical limits. In 1942, after Carl dropped to ninety-three pounds, his doctor diagnosed an advanced case of TB in both lungs. He sent Carl away from his beloved city, his wife, and his young son to the state sanatorium in Norwich. This was in the days before wonder drugs; the only cure was bed rest.

Despite following doctor's orders, Carl didn't get well quickly. Months went by, and the doctor finally agreed to give Carl a pass to go home for Christmas. During his leave Carl took his

boy Dickie to see a department store Santa. But Carl was disappointed in Santa's surroundings, and when he returned to the sanatorium he began to plan a special Santaland for the children of Torrington. Carl had several setbacks in his recovery, but after four years he finally went home and returned to his job at the Recreation Department. And in 1947 Carl's dream came true when Christmas Village opened at Alvord Playground. A one-room Tudor house became Santa's Throne Room; another little house is Santa's workshop. Santa's reindeer reside in a stable in the back.

These days Santa's helpers spend weeks preparing for his visit. Gus Lucia, a Street and Parks Department employee, looks forward to it all year. They call Gus Mr. Christmas Village because he's worked on it for more than a decade. As you might imagine, Gus says, "Christmas is my favorite time of year."

Gus stacks Santa's workshop from top to bottom with toys, rewiring the ones that use batteries and then hiding control wires in a secret panel. He stands by when the kids stream into the room so he can make the toys come to life. "If they're looking at something that's not moving and you start that toy moving, their eyes light up," he says as his do, too. Gus gets a kick out of the children, maybe because they remind him of his own visits as a boy. "Being as little as I was, I thought it was a big town and a magical village."

Some of the toys that delighted Gus as a child are still here. Each year the hottest doll of the season is added to the display. Favorite playthings of the last fifty years populate the workshop.

Next door, Jim Sica decks out Santa's Throne Room with more decorations than you can count and yards of garland. A warm fire is burning in the fireplace as each child sits on Santa's knee and receives a gift to take home.

Jim loves watching the kids' reactions. "Some of them are scared," he says, "and they cry or holler. Some are in awe, and they don't say much."

Some are a little reluctant to tell Santa what they're hoping to find under the tree. When Santa asks Melissa Russo what she would like for Christmas, she speaks to the jolly old elf in the tiniest voice. "I wrote some things down on my list," she whispers.

Santa asks, "Did you mail it to Mrs. Claus?" When Melissa nods, he tells her, "Good, then I should have it in plenty of time for Christmas."

Many of these parents came to Santa's Throne Room when they were kids, including Lori Binstadt, who grew up in Litchfield. "It makes Christmas really special for the kids, and for me," she says. "It feels like you are really at Santa's village and the North Pole."

That would have made Carl Bozenski very happy. Carl survived another bout with tuberculosis in the 1950s, but he died in a car accident in 1986. In his honor the name of his special creation is officially Carl Bozenski's Christmas Village.

Santa is in Torrington for two weeks a year, but the spirit of generosity lingers all season, thanks to a local man who had a very big heart—Carl Bozenski.

Playthings of the Past

The Wilton Heritage Museum has displayed playthings of the past at Christmastime for thirty years. Volunteer curator Mary Lou Logan is a collector, restorer, and lecturer in the field of dolls, dollhouses, and toys. She has helped the historical society put together a permanent collection that is impressive for a small museum. Steiff animals fill one case and include a large kangaroo, an alligator, and a seal. A family of Raggedy Ann and Andy dolls, created by Norwalk illustrator and

 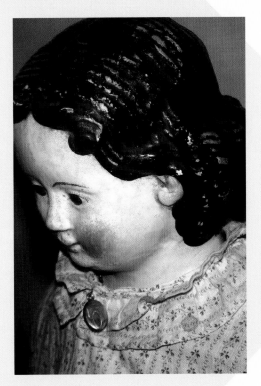

author Johnny Gruelle, takes up residence in another case. Vintage dolls and toys from the nineteenth and early twentieth centuries introduce kids to what toys were like before electronics and computers. Society members also put together an extensive layout of moving and stationary trains of all gauges. All this is on view during December and January at the Betts-Sturges-Blackmar House.

Chocolate Lace

Just as every snowflake is different, so is every piece of a confection called Chocolate Lace. And in fact, snow inspired the creation of this treat. In turn-of-the-twentieth-century Russia, a little girl named Eugenia Tay would boil sugar into syrup, take it outside, and drizzle it in a lacy pattern on the snow. When it had hardened, she'd bring it back inside and dip it in chocolate.

"When the communists came into power, Eugenia left the country with her family. They continued the tradition, but in New York City they poured the syrup on a cold marble slab instead of on snow," says Steve Bray, now owner of Chocolate Lace. "I guess the idea of New York snow and drizzling anything on it is not particularly appetizing," he laughs.

Maybe its origins in snow are what make Chocolate Lace popular at the holidays, though these days it's made year-round.

Eugenia's candy became so popular in New York that she built a business selling it. By the 1920s she had cultivated so many customers that she invented a machine to make the candy so she could keep up with the demand.

Steve Bray left his job as a marketing manager with a big corporation to buy the Chocolate Lace company and Eugenia's antique machine, which he then nicknamed. "We ended up with Veronica, for Veronica Lace, a takeoff on the old movie star, Veronica Lake, who had the bangs coming down over her forehead."

In a one-room factory, the candy man, Carlos, melts sugar and corn syrup in an enormous copper pot. When it caramelizes, he pours the syrup into the machine and it feeds into two separate dishes, one of which dances over the parallel lines created by the other. Then the sugary web is bathed in chocolate. It comes out looking like what one fan called "the work of a drunken spider." The sweet scent permeating the place is enough to intoxicate a chocoholic. At the height of production, gearing up for the Christmas season, about a dozen people work in the plant in Bethel.

Steve's wife, Connie, works in the business too, but says she has about gotten her fill of sweets. Now she saves her sampling for special occasions and dinner parties, when she often serves coffee ice cream with Dark Chocolate Lace crumbled over it.

The company is unusual in that it's the *only* one in the world making its particular product—a claim few firms can make. Steve says, "What a pleasure to know you are making something not only unique, but so marvelous."

Chocolate Lace comes in six flavors: Dark Chocolate, Mint Dark Chocolate, Milk Chocolate Toasted Almond, Cappuccino, Rum, and Grand Marnier. A seven-ounce box retails for about ten dollars, while a fourteen-ounce box sells for about sixteen dollars. It's found in gourmet shops all over the country, but Chocolate Lace is a treat made *only* in Connecticut.

The Chocolate Factory

Christmas comes early at the Thompson Candy Company in Meriden. While the rest of us are thinking beach and barbecue, Santa Claus is coming to town at the 122-year-old chocolate maker.

Not just one Santa, but thousands and thousands of chocolate Santas march along a conveyor belt from molding to wrapping. Forty-two million mini-chocolate ornaments and a couple of million bells and other chocolate treats will be shipped around the world, according to Jeff White, the owner and president of Thompson Candy Company. In a year Thompson molds ten million pounds of chocolate into sweet novelties. The chocolate they use is made in New Jersey, according to Jeff's secret recipe.

"In places like Ohio they like a very milky chocolate, and in New England we like a darker chocolate," Jeff says, "so we've tried to come up with something that's somewhere in the middle."

Thompson candy is coveted not only for its taste, but also for old-fashioned decorative touches like hand-tied bows on the wrappings. Jeff says Thompson is the only U.S. candy company with national distribution that still prizes handwork. It was nurtured by three generations of Thompsons and two generations of Whites. While modern technology turns out vast numbers of pieces, Thompson still has room for a hand molding division because Jeff believes, "Chocolate that's done by hand doesn't taste the same as chocolate that's done by machine."

That's why Helga Hoxihe makes pecan bark the same way it's been made here since 1879, using her hands to spread warm dark chocolate in a waxed-paper-lined tray and fold in pounds of pecans. Despite her apron and gloves, Helga is covered in chocolate to her elbows, but she doesn't mind. "It doesn't bother me anymore, but when I first started that was a different story," she says. "Every day I told myself, *This is the last day, there's no way I'm gonna come back.*" She chuckles. "That was two and a half years ago."

Some employees have worked here for decades, since the days when Jeff's dad owned the business. One reason might be the perks. "We allow the employees to eat all they want," Jeff says as he smiles, and admits that he is a bit of a chocoholic. He even met his wife while she was working behind a candy counter.

Thompson makes more than four hundred items, including a complete Christmas line of foil-wrapped ornaments, Santas, snowmen of all sizes, and even little chocolate nutcrackers. Thompson Candy Company in Meriden is a chocolate lover's haven where the holidays are extra sweet.

Right: A chocolate-lover's heaven in Guilford.

Step inside the church hall at St. George's Episcopal Church in Middlebury and your nose will lead you to the room where an elaborate village has sprung up—a gingerbread village.

Marilyn Terrell remembers when the first such gingerbread village was built here more than thirty years ago. It fit on a card table. "Now it takes up a whole room," she says, leading us on a tour of a make-believe community with sixty-five buildings made from the pungent cookie dough, united by paths paved in poppy seed and lined with kidney bean walkways.

"Everything is edible. That's the only rule," she explains. After that, the construction crew can let their imaginations run wild. Parishioners magically transform sugar and spice into edible art.

There's an airport, a lighthouse, and a ski chalet crafted from gingerbread. So is a castle where Saint George is valiantly slaying the dragon. A pirate ship sails a glossy blue sea made of melted-down lollipops, and a tiny stand sells Christmas trees crafted from ice cream cones.

Gumdrop penguins with wings made of Necco wafers strap on sticks of Juicy Fruit gum for skis, while pretzel reindeer venture out of the forest.

"You'd be surprised how hard those reindeer are to make," Silvana Lessack confides. "You have to break the pretzels *just so* to make antlers." Silvana is one of the fifty parishioners who helped build the village. Her nine-year-old daughter Amanda created a pet shop, inhabited by painted animal crackers looking for a good home.

A tough-looking marzipan mutt named Spike guards Bub's Garage, outfitted with licorice jumper cables and fingernail-sized hubcaps made of marzipan. Across town, intricately decorated marzipan teapots barely as big as a cherry pit are at the ready should some elfin customer want a cup of tea and a croissant.

Marilyn says the gingerbread builders, who range in age from three to eighty-three, are always on the lookout for candies that might be contrived into cunning bits of trim. Dentyne chewing gum is stacked like bricks with cake frosting for mortar. Broken bits of Jolly Rancher

candies form stained-glass windows for the church.

Marilyn Terrell says the gingerbread builders who gather on Thanksgiving weekend to erect the village are "always thinking about next year. We visit every candy store in town, and wherever we go."

That's because each year the village is an entirely new creation. It takes more than three hundred pounds of flour, ten cases of confectioner's sugar and twenty-five pounds of granulated sugar, ten gallons of molasses, three pounds each of ginger and nutmeg, combined with four pounds of powdered meringue and fifty pounds of margarine to construct the scene. Practically the entire parish is involved, and it's not unusual to find three generations in one family laboring over their creation.

Each year there's a theme. In 2000 it was Millennium Dreams, and one wag included a voting booth in a nod to the disputed presidential election. Before Christmas ever comes, Marilyn Terrell is already thinking about next year's village and recruiting her "construction crew."

The gingerbread village is on display for one week each year on the first Saturday in December and is open to the public. School groups and seniors arrive by the busload. Admission is free, yet every gingerbread house is for sale—and some fetch more than a hundred dollars. The exhibit has grown into the church's biggest fund-raiser.

Gingerbread Dough and Royal Icing

Gingerbread artist Teresa Layman of Warren shares the recipes she uses for all her creations.

6¾ cups flour	1½ cups light corn syrup
1 tablespoon cinnamon	1¼ cups packed light brown sugar
1½ teaspoons ginger	1 cup margarine
½ teaspoon salt	

Cut nonstick baking parchment to fit your baking sheet. Stir together the dry ingredients in a large bowl. Combine the light corn syrup, brown sugar, and margarine in a 2-quart saucepan. Stir constantly over medium heat until the margarine is melted. Pour the syrup mixture into the flour mixture. Stir well, using your hands to mix as the dough becomes stiff. If you are using a heavy-duty KitchenAid mixer, the mixer can handle this dough; lightweight mixers cannot. Chill the dough 1 hour or until it is about room temperature.

Preheat oven to 350°F. Roll out the dough on nonstick baking parchment to a thickness of ⅛". Using the patterns of your choice, cut out the necessary pieces. Bake 12 to 15 minutes or until golden brown. Smaller pieces should be baked separately from larger ones, as baking times will vary depending on size. Check for air bubbles during baking and poke them with a knife or skewer. When baking is done, slide the parchment with the hot gingerbread onto a cooling rack. Make sure all the pieces lie flat.

When the pieces are cool, assemble them with Royal Icing:

> 1 pound confectioners' sugar
> 3 egg whites, at room temperature (use large eggs, not jumbo eggs)
> ⅛ teaspoon cream of tartar

Sift the confectioners' sugar. Place the egg whites in a mixer bowl. Add the sugar and cream of tartar to egg whites while stirring. When all the sugar is incorporated, turn the mixer to high and beat the mixture until thick and very white. The icing should hold a stiff peak. The process takes about 5 to 7 minutes, longer if you are using a hand-held mixer. Cover the icing tightly with plastic wrap, as it dries very quickly. Use paste food colors to tint the icing. A tiny dot on a toothpick to a quarter cup of icing will make a nice pastel color—but be sure to add it a little at a time. With practice you will learn how much to use to get the color intensity you want.

The Teddy Bear Tea at the Florence Griswold Museum in Old Lyme.

Winter Wonderland

For our first Christmas in our new home, my husband Tom and I were inspired by the cathedral ceiling in the great room to find a fir tree that would flirt with its fifteen-foot height and scent the whole house with piney fragrance. A few weeks before Christmas, we bundled up in fleece scarves and ski parkas, packed our rusty but trusty saw, and headed to the H. Smith Richardson Sanctuary in Westport, operated as a Christmas tree farm by the Connecticut Audubon Society. We trudged through a frozen field, our toes tingling with the cold, rejecting one tree after another. Then we spied it. A proud balsam stood solitary and majestic on a knoll at the far end of the field. Its lofty branches would shelter dozens of our prized ornaments, collected over our twelve years together. When we stood right next to it, gazing up at an abandoned bird's nest in one of its branches, I knew it was a tree we would long remember.

Just as Tom started to make the first cut in its thick trunk, I asked tentatively, "You're sure it's not *too* tall?"

"No," he said. "It will be perfect."

When it took two extra people to help us lug it to the parking lot, I began to feel apprehensive, but Tom wasn't concerned. "It just looks big out here without anything to give perspective."

We paid for the tree, feeling good that our donation would help support the Audubon Society, but when the two assistants found that the tree was too long to tie to the top of the car, I was worried. "No problem," they said, "we deliver." I should have backed out then, but the light in Tom's eyes reminded me of a boy finding that shiny new bike under the tree on Christmas morning.

That afternoon when the pickup truck pulled into our driveway, I was engrossed in decorating a tabletop tree, barely a foot tall, with tiny ornaments no bigger than your thumbnail. When three young men, plus Tom, came around the back of the house with our Christmas tree, I had some perspective all right. That tree was *never* going to fit into our house! It took all four men to drag it in. They squeezed it through the sliding doors and started to straighten it. The tree's top scraped the ceiling, and still it was bent over. Not only was this behemoth more than eighteen feet tall, but it was broad enough to fill the room nearly from wall to wall. "Take it outside and do something with it," I suggested with a note of panic in my voice. They puffed and strained and pulled it out into the yard, and as I concentrated on my Lilliputian tree, I heard the whine of a chain saw. A little off the top, a little off the bottom, and a shearing all around, and soon they had it back inside, commanding the space in a way no other tree has.

It took every ornament we had to fill that tree, and then some. It was so enormous that we hung full-sized toys from some of its branches to take up space. We had to turn sideways to shimmy past it. We made three trips to the Christmas shop for more lights, more than a thousand in all. But I was right about one thing. It was a Christmas tree we will never forget.

Left: A star glows in Canton. Above right: A pensive moment in a sleigh, Torrington.

All Spruced Up

When Al Amundsen bought *Wrights Mill Farm* in Canterbury in 1970, he was just looking for a peaceful country home in a quiet location. "I really wasn't thinking of farming. I had just started practicing orthodontia, and was busy with offices in Storrs and Putnam and on Nantucket," he says. The farm, which dates back to the late 1600s, had a homestead built in 1758 by Jedediah Benjamin. Because of the hydropower generated by a pond and steeply dropping brook, the farm had been the site of two gristmills and a sawmill, and some of their remnants were still visible in the woods.

"The land had not been farmed since the Civil War, and it was run-down and overgrown," Al remembers. When he cleared some of the trees and sold the timber, he didn't expect to be one of the state's bigger tree farms some thirty years later. But today Wrights Mill grows thousands of trees in ten varieties of spruce and fir.

Al and his wife, Amanda, started out with forty acres, but bought two hundred more when a neighbor, who had planned to open a golf course, passed away without realizing his dream. "I thought that much land ought to be productive," Al says, so he started raising Christmas trees. It was a crop he knew something about, since his father had cultivated a small crop of trees when he was a boy.

"I started to notice that on my trips to my office in Nantucket I was becoming envious of my friends there in the tourism business," says Al. He eventually sold his orthodontia practices and turned Wrights Mill Farm into more than just a place to cut your Christmas tree—it's now a favorite family holiday outing. Kids and their parents pile into horse-drawn and tractor-drawn hayrides, enjoy caroling and live music, drink hot cocoa, and spend a little time with Santa and his elves.

Inside an antique barn the Amundsens operate the Silo Christmas Shop, selling locally made and imported ornaments, gifts, and wreaths. Visitors climb to the top of the silo and enjoy the tranquil views of the farm from the observatory.

Although the actual selling season for trees is short, families start showing up to tag their special trees just after Labor Day. That led the Amundsens to think about their farm as a year-round destination. Today they host picnics, parties, and weddings in an outdoor pavilion and a four-seasons lodge on their farm. Hot-air ballooning is a new attraction, available at certain times of year.

At another family attraction—the *Jones Family Farms*, nestled in the White Hills of Shelton—harvesting your own Christmas tree has been a tradition for sixty years. Phillip Hubbell Jones started growing trees in the 1930s as a 4-H project. More than one hundred thousand trees grow on the farm's two hundred acres of hillsides. All cut-your-own trees are forty-five dollars regardless of size, and a collectible, dated ornament made by Woodbury Pewter is your gift from the Jones family with each tree. The farm also offers freshly harvested trees in the barnyard, and wreaths and garland in the Sawmill Barn. The Holiday Gatherings Farm Gift Shop in a former dairy barn sells ornaments, vintage oddities, farm-grown herbal products, and lots of craft items, mostly made by Jones family members. Hot mulled cider and fresh-baked cookies are a must after cutting your tree, and a stop at the bonfire will warm you up.

The farm has been in the family since Philip James Jones, a Welsh Irish immigrant, began working the land in the 1850s. Five generations later the family says it is still "preserving old-fashioned values of farmers—stewardship of the land, a love of plants and animals, and a life in harmony with the seasons." Jones Family Farms has been named by *Yankee* magazine as one of the outstanding reasons to visit New England.

Previous page: James A. Fazzone's Cheshire CT Tree Farm; this page above, Smith Tree Farm in Guilford; at left, Jones Family Farms in Shelton.

More Christmas Trees

Cutting your own Christmas tree has become more and more popular in Connecticut. "Twenty years ago, most trees sold here came from Canada and northern New England," says Al Amundsen of Wrights Mill Farm. "These days a lot of people who have some acreage think it would be nice to grow a crop that they could make some money on, so they have planted trees."

There are dozens of other tree farms across Connecticut. To find out more, call the Connecticut Christmas Tree Growers Association (see Resources). The Connecticut State Nursery, located in Voluntown, is the source of over a million tree and shrub seedlings annually. Seedlings are available to landowners in Connecticut; for information, again, see Resources.

Jones Family Farms in Shelton; inset photo: Smith Tree Farm, Guilford.

A Passion for Poinsettias

Christmas in August? That's when University of Connecticut plant science professor Richard McAvoy fills his greenhouse with poinsettias, more than 120 varieties of them. But, Richard says, stop by for a visit in late summer, and you might not recognize the traditional blooms of winter.

"They are all green until October. Early in November they show a hint of color," he says, "but they don't reveal their full color until closer to the holiday. In nature they turn color when the length of the day is less than twelve hours and twenty minutes."

And these days their "full color" may not be the traditional crimson. "Twenty or thirty years ago, there were a handful of varieties," says Richard. "But in the 1990s there was an explosion. Now there are hundreds of varieties of poinsettias."

Poinsettias now range in color from a purple variety known as 'Plum Pudding' to a bright yellow known as 'Lemon Drop' and include a rainbow of reds, pinks, and peaches, not to mention salmon, orange, cream, and white. Variegated varieties like 'Monet' and 'Jingle Bells' are increasingly popular. While they once grew wild in Mexico as a shrub, poinsettias now vary in size from dwarves—just a few inches tall—to trees. Some don't even look like poinsettias. The newer 'Winter Rose' types resemble peonies. The colored leaves of the poinsettia plant are in fact bracts, not petals. The actual flower of the poinsettia looks like a small bunch of berries in the center of a cluster of bracts.

'Plum Pudding' surrounded by other new varieties in the UConn greenhouse.

So given all the choices, how does a nursery decide which poinsettias will please Connecticut customers? That's where Professor McAvoy comes in. He runs the UConn poinsettia trial—nurturing varieties provided by major wholesalers from other states as a service to commercial greenhouse growers from across Connecticut. The UConn poinsettia trial gives local growers a chance to see the different plants side by side and to evaluate them for color, height, hardiness, and other qualities. UConn also gets consumers' opinions on new plants. This information is important in a very competitive market. An official report on agriculture in New England estimated that more than a million poinsettias were raised in Connecticut in 1999, but McAvoy says the real number may be twice that.

The poinsettia is native to Central America and Mexico, and was introduced to this country by the first U.S. ambassador to Mexico. Andrew Jackson appointed Joel Roberts Poinsett to the post in the 1820s. Although he is said to have had a distinguished diplomatic career, Poinsett is remembered best for the cuttings he brought back and grew in his South Carolina greenhouse. If he visited the UConn greenhouses today, Poinsett might not recognize the plant that bears his name.

The many varieties of poinsettias, clockwise from top left: 'Monet Twilight', 'Silverstar Red', 'Monet', 'Carousel', 'Marblestar', and 'Orion Red'.

The plants and greenery of
Christmas, clockwise from
top right: the Greenbrier
Greenhouse at Edgerton
Park, New Haven; tiny
topiaries; Gilbertie's Herb
Farm, Westport; amaryllis,
a holiday favorite; wreath-
making workshop at Wilbur
& King Nurseries, Guilford;
a simple tabletop tree.

Ice Harvest

Today a frozen pond is an invitation for a skating party. In the days before refrigeration, however, ice was a precious commodity, harvested on local lakes and ponds in December, January, and February. Occasionally local historical societies re-create an ice harvest using antique tools and techniques, to the delight of local residents and tourists.

One such reenacted ice harvest takes place on Lake Waramaug in New Preston, where ice was big business in the early twentieth century. The reenactment brought out old-timers who remember the days when they cut ice for local dairy farmers to cool their milk.

The harvest starts with an ice plow, dragged across the surface to score the ice. Then a four-foot-long saw with jagged teeth slices through the ice, which by January can be fifteen inches thick. Cakes of ice are chopped loose, floated down a channel carved into the lake, and speared by a man with a pike. Each heavy cake is loaded onto a sled and dragged by a team of oxen to an icehouse, where it's packed in sawdust and stored.

It used to take resident Glen Spargo three days to fill his icehouse. He recalls, "You probably had 150 men on the crew, some on the lake, and some in the icehouse, which had eight rooms. Five or six men in each room stacked the ice as it came in."

Until the late 1930s, the Shepaug Litchfield & Northern Railroad shipped much of that ice to New York City. These days it's more likely to be turned into a fanciful creation by a local chef with a talent for ice carving and appreciative restaurant clients. And only one small icehouse still stands on the shore of Lake Waramaug—a reminder of winter days long ago.

Let it snow! Clockwise from top left: Chester, Orange, Middlefield, Danbury, New Britain, Derby, Branford, Southington, Middletown (center).

Dashing through the Snow

It's a scene right out of a Currier and Ives print: a coachman cloaked in bearskin, a Victorian lady in a bonnet, and a horse-drawn sleigh. But this is reality, at least at John and Kate Allegra's fantasy farm in East Haddam, imbued with the character of another era.

John and Kate don't reminisce much about the past. They don't have to, because they live it. In their business and their working museum, they've revived an era when a snowstorm didn't shut down interstate highways, because there weren't any. At Allegra Farm, a snowfall means a chance to hitch up the matched pair of Arabians, bundle up in bearskin, and set off into the lovely countryside.

John has restored a fleet of carriages and sleighs. Kate collects the vintage costumes that help set the mood. John tells visitors, "This is as close as you'll ever get to the real thing, because it is the real thing." And for us passengers all wrapped up under buffalo lap robes, with snow flying under the blades of the sleigh, it's enough to make us feel like singing. And pretty soon we are, breaking into a hearty chorus of "Jingle Bells."

The sleigh winds its way through the fields and woods. As twilight draws near, romance often warms the wintry air. John recalls, "We've actually had people propose in sleighs in the middle of a blizzard. I'm always hoping she'll say yes, and there haven't been any yet that have gone astray." Maybe that's because it was a sleigh that brought John and Kate together. They met at an auction in Pennsylvania back in the days when they each ran their own carriage companies.

Kate laughs, "We ended up bidding on the same sleigh and he got it, but he had to pay a lot more!" John laughs, too. "She got one and I got one, and now we have them both," he says. And Kate adds, "I got him!"

The Allegras' shared passion for the past led them to build a twelve-thousand-square-foot barn, gleaming with snow-white paint and decked in pine roping. It's handcrafted in post-and-beam construction, made from hemlock that is native to the area. Inside one of the country's largest authentic livery stables is the Horse Drawn Carriage and Sleigh Museum of New England, one of the few places where you can not only view but also ride in the nineteenth-century carriages, coaches, and sleighs.

The barn is filled with memorabilia, carriages, coaches, sleighs, and even two horse-drawn hearses. Visitors can watch as John restores carriages, repairs antique harnesses, and re-creates carriage wheels.

The Allegras generally run sleigh rides every day as long as there is snow. They'll even build a campfire for you, if you're hardy enough to plan a winter picnic. When there is no snow, they offer carriage, coach, and hayrides.

John clearly enjoys the work. "We meet a lot of special people. We make dreams come true, and that's what it's all about."

His passengers couldn't agree more after a sleigh ride into the past.

Sleigh Bells Ring

What would the holiday season be without the sounds of bells? Jingling sleigh bells, tolling church bells, and the peals of hand bells are sounds that define Christmas. In the late 1800s the bell-making capital of the world was East Hampton, Connecticut, where bell makers produced ninety percent of the world's sleigh bells. Today Bevin Brothers Manufacturing Company still makes two hundred varieties of bells in an old brick factory building there. Stanley Bevin traces his company back to 1830 and says proudly, "We are the oldest family-owned manufacturing firm in the state." They were also one of the first companies in Connecticut to make toys. Besides sleigh bells Bevin makes decorative bells to hang on Christmas trees, brass hand bells, copper cowbells, and lots of special orders. Stanley says they've even outfitted Santa with bells for his reindeer. "We like to think that we've definitely contributed to the joy that Santa spreads."

Ahead of Her Time

Frances Osborne Kellogg was a woman ahead of her time. When her father died in 1907, the probate judge urged Fanny and her mother to sell the businesses that Wilbur Fisk Osborne had built up. After all, he reasoned, women didn't run companies, and there was no male heir. But Fanny didn't take his advice. Instead, at the age of thirty-one, she took over the family businesses, and within a year they had grown even more profitable.

"She did find it difficult in the beginning to conduct business, being the sole businesswoman in the valley," says Will Stoddard, the former director of the Osborne Homestead Museum in Derby. "She succeeded because of her determination."

Fanny's formal education had ended abruptly at the age of sixteen, when she lost the vision in one eye following an accident, but her love for learning, music, and literature lived on. She often invited friends to Osbornedale, her home and estate, for lectures and performances by some of the most interesting people of the day. Aviatrix Amelia Earhart, for instance, visited two months before her disappearance.

At forty-three Fanny married Waldo Stewart Kellogg, a New York architect. Waldo became interested in the family dairy herd and bred Holstein cows. The dairy farm, adjacent to the house,

Snowdrifts on a barn in North Madison.

is now the four-hundred-acre Osbornedale State Park and the site of the Kellogg Environmental Center. In winter its rolling hills and meadows attract snowshoers and cross-country skiers. There's ice skating on Pickett's Pond and a pavilion for warming up. Guided bird walks are offered throughout the season.

The Colonial-revival house itself is especially beautiful at the holidays. Five Naugatuck Valley garden clubs decorate it with floral arrangements and holiday displays that complement Fanny's European antiques, her porcelain collection, and the gleaming silver pieces made by one of her own companies. "We don't have Fanny's collection of ornaments, though I wish we did," says museum educator Christiana Ferraro. "But we do know a little bit about how she celebrated the holidays. She was a big supporter of the Derby Methodist church and helped ensure that there would always be glorious music there at Christmas."

In the living room, Fanny's rare leather-bound and gilt-trimmed third edition of *A Christmas Carol* by Charles Dickens is placed on a table, and the holiday decorations—including English "crackers"—reflect the time period. Waldo's studio is decorated with a favorite Victorian luxury: candied fruit sparkling with crystals of sugar.

In the Milk Room, where Waldo stored his farm records and hung portraits of prize-winning cows on the walls, a Christmas tree is decorated with felt farm animals. "Although Fanny had no children of her own, she was generous with the children of her farmhands, making sure a little girl had a doll at Christmas, a little boy a truck or another toy," says Christiana.

Poinsettias, amaryllis, and cyclamen brighten the house, and other flowers are chosen for their meaning. "Victorians believed in the secret language of flowers, and that different flowers imparted different messages," says Christiana.

After touring the home, you may want to join a workshop at the Kellogg Environmental Center to learn how to replicate some of the decorations you've seen—from wreaths to confectionary houses. Outdoor crafts are emphasized at the center, too, with workshops on recycled gift-wrapping and how to adorn your landscape with ornaments that birds and other wildlife can snack on.

One of the most accomplished women of her day, Frances Osborne Kellogg willed her home, her farm, and her holiday hospitality to the people of Connecticut.

A Fine Feathered Christmas

A common holiday tradition in earlier times was known as the Christmas Side Hunt. People would choose sides and go into the field with their guns; whichever team brought back the largest numbers of birds won. But on Christmas Day 1900, Frank Chapman, a member of the newly formed Audubon Society, began a new tradition that has taken its place. Chapman's idea was not to kill birds, but count them. Both the conservation movement and the Christmas Bird Count have taken off since then.

Connecticut was part of that first count, and bird lovers in Connecticut continue to count our feathered friends to this day. In 1900 twenty-seven people counted birds in twenty-five areas, or "circles," as they are designated by the Audubon Society. About 18,500 individual birds were counted, mostly in the northeastern part of North America. In the 101st Christmas Bird Count, more than forty-five thousand Americans in 1,846 circles counted more than fifty-four million individual birds! It's not uncommon for birders in Connecticut to record a hundred species inland during the Christmas Bird Count, and more on the shoreline. Recently a record number of wild turkeys was recorded in the Hartford area, and birders found two snowy owls, something of a rarity in the state.

Birders like to say that when they toast the New Year with champagne at midnight, they are already dreaming of another year of birding and the unusual species they might spot in the next twelve months. Bird- and wildlife-watching is a growing hobby in the state, with more than three-quarters of a million people in Connecticut calling themselves wildlife-watchers.

Winter along the shore, clockwise from top left: Westport, Southport, Norwalk, Stony Creek, Stony Creek, Southport, Stonington Borough (center).

Reindeer Games

At Christmastime, years ago when I was a young reporter, I visited the legendary Tin Pan Alley and the renowned songwriter Johnny Marks. He wasn't well then and his glory days of songwriting were behind him, but he sat down at the piano and sang me the original version of "Rudolph the Red-Nosed Reindeer," the song he wrote for Gene Autry and later reworked for the TV special starring Burl Ives.

Johnny was asked to write "Rudolph" by his brother-in-law, Robert L. May, a copywriter with the Montgomery Ward department store chain. May had written the story of the lovable reindeer with the shiny nose, and Ward's had already given away millions of illustrated copies of the story before Johnny Marks ever came up with a single note. Still, the song eventually sold more than thirty million records and inspired the TV special that debuted in 1964 and still airs today. The prolific songwriter shared a few of his other holiday hits with me that rainy afternoon in his sheet-music-crammed office in New York City, including "Rockin' Around the Christmas Tree," "A Holly Jolly Christmas," "When Santa Gets Your Letter," and "Silver and Gold." Johnny Marks died about a year later, and I think of him every time I hear "Rudolph the Red-Nosed Reindeer."

Heather (above) and with her friend, Beardsley Zoo educator Linda Tomas.

The Beardsley Park Zoo is a good place to learn about the animal that inspired the story and song. Every year the magical animals from the holiday tale are on display through the month of December. The Reindeer Encounter is particularly enjoyable for small children, who will also like the crafts and coloring opportunities.

For adults, the zoo educators offer more information about reindeer than you could use up in a lifetime of holiday cocktail party chatter. For instance, did you know that reindeer are remarkably similar to caribou? Or that the indigenous people of Norway, known as the Sami, actually domesticate reindeer and use them to pull sleds?

More reindeer fun facts: Both males and females have antlers, and no two sets of antlers are identical. Nor are they symmetrical. Reindeer do not have any top front teeth, and they are cud chewers. They are smaller than most people imagine, standing only four feet tall at the shoulder. If snow lands on the animal's back, it will not melt due to a protective layer of guard hairs on the reindeer's winter coat.

And think of this the next time you read the story of Rudolph to your little ones: Santa's reindeer have different names in different cultures. Although we know them as Comet, Cupid, Donner, Blitzen, Dancer, Prancer, Dasher, and Vixen (and Rudolph of course), stories in other countries call the reindeer pulling Kris Kringle's sleigh Twilight, Tundra, Bramble, Lichen, Windswept, Heather, Snowball, and Crag.

Spirit of the Season

As a little girl I once asked my dad, "Is there really a Santa Claus?"

"Of course there is," he assured me. "You don't think Dad and Mom can afford all these toys for five kids, do you?" That was pretty persuasive at the time.

And I still believe in Santa Claus. I know he exists because I see him everywhere. He may not live at the North Pole or look like the Santa you see at the mall, wearing a red plush suit and a long white beard, but he truly has Santa's spirit of generosity and love.

Sometimes the Santa who lives among us is an older gentleman with white hair and rosy cheeks—like Eric Hultgren, the toyman. Eric delivers his handmade wooden toys not just on Christmas Eve, but all year long to the sick children at Bridgeport Hospital. Sometimes these real-life Santas are women, like Barbara Bellinger, who opens her lovely Tudor home to host an elegant holiday tea party that raises money to help women fight breast cancer. Sometimes Santa arrives not in a sleigh powered by eight tiny reindeer, but in a Bell Jet Ranger helicopter, the way George Morgan does when he takes time every Christmas to recognize the dedicated service of our coastline's lighthouse keepers.

What motivates these real-life Santas? What infuses them with such a superabundance of holiday spirit? Sometimes giving to others is a way of overcoming loss, as it is for Eric, who started making toys while his wife was seriously ill. Sometimes they are moved by thankfulness, as in Barbara Bellinger's case. A breast cancer survivor, she is grateful that she will live to see another Christmas, her favorite time of year. Sometimes it's for the pure joy of seeing a smile on the face of a child, as it is for the Bike Man, Chuck Graeb, who longed for a bike when he was a boy. That dream eluded him, but it's a dream he can make come true for other kids today.

So Santa may not be a jolly old elf in a fur-trimmed red suit. Santa's spirit is surely in Julie Hurlburt, who helps cook a community dinner for three hundred of the lonely and homeless in Middletown. Santa may be the woman at work who organizes a giving tree so needy children will have gifts on Christmas morning. Santa may wear a Marine Corps uniform and collect thousands of toys to give away in the poorest parts of town. Santa may be the friend who calls you in the middle of the holiday rush and urges you to slow down, at least for an hour, and come to church, enjoy a Christmas concert, and meditate on the real meaning of Christmas. In Connecticut, you don't have to look far to find Santa. His spirit is all around you.

A holiday message at Hubbard Park in Meriden, above;
at left, the spirit of the season in Colebrook.

A Cup of Christmas Tea

It's easy to see why you would serve a formal tea in a house like Barbara and George Bellinger's. The imposing Tudor home in Bridgeport's Stratfield historic district dates back to 1929, when that's what polite society did. The home has an elegance that recalls an earlier age—with tinted leaded-glass windows, dark wooden floors, and the initials of its first owner crafted into the metal grillwork.

When Barbara Bellinger moved into the house a decade ago, she remembers thinking, *This is a winter house. This is a Christmas house.* Barbara's daughter Monique Jackson says Christmas is very important to Barbara: "She does have a chip in her brain that's always on Christmas."

So every year Barbara and George haul a twelve-foot tree home to hold court in their living room. Barbara decorates the house with her collection of African-American Santas. A balcony overlooking the living room is the perfect place for a chamber group to play classical music, and the lovely strains of Christmas carols greet the guests arriving for Barbara's annual Christmas tea.

Soon eighty people are merrily circulating through the dining room, where silver epergnes hold long stems of crimson roses, red satin ribbons dangle from the brass chandelier, and squares of gingerbread with dollops of ginger cream are stacked beside bite-sized scones spread with English jam and clotted cream. There are tea sandwiches stuffed with almond chicken, watercress, and cucumber, and chocolate toffee trifle served by young women in lace-trimmed pinafores over candy-cane-striped skirts. A fine Darjeeling tea blended by Harney and Sons in Salisbury is steeping in a china teapot. The tea is catered by Carol Timpanelli, a dear friend of Barbara's, whose Royal Tea Company has catered for Martha Stewart, the duchess of York, and fashion designer Tommy Hilfiger. Shortbread cookies shaped like Christmas trees are stacked on a three-tiered silver tea tray. Each cookie is threaded with a fine satin ribbon.

"Those wishing cookies are my trademark," says Carol. "You eat the cookie, then tie the ribbon around your finger, make a wish, and it's guaranteed to come true."

Barbara Bellinger's wish came true. In 1997 she was diagnosed with breast cancer. After two surgeries, radiation, and chemotherapy, Barbara is now cancer-free or, as she puts it, "clean, blessed and thankful."

That's why the annual tea is now more than a gathering of friends. They come together not only to celebrate the Christmas season, but also to celebrate Barbara's life and to support the

Norma T. Pfriem Breast Cancer Center at Bridgeport Hospital, where Barbara serves on the board. She added this responsibility to her already busy life and career as a vice president at People's Bank because "we have to make up our minds we won't be defeated by cancer."

At her own favorite time of year, Barbara Bellinger is ensuring that other women will live to celebrate another Christmas, too.

Royal Trifle

from the Royal Tea Company, Trumbull

10 TO 12 SERVINGS

1½ ounces unsweetened chocolate, finely chopped
1 cup sifted cake flour
1 teaspoon baking soda
¼ teaspoon salt
1¾ cups (packed) golden brown sugar
½ cup (1 stick) unsalted butter, room temperature
1 large egg

1 large egg yolk
¼ cup buttermilk
½ cup boiling water
1 teaspoon vanilla extract
3 cups chilled whipping cream
1½ cups chocolate-covered English toffee bits (two 6-ounce bags)
Semisweet chocolate shavings

Preheat the oven to 375°F. Butter and flour a 9-inch-square baking pan with 2-inch-high sides. Melt the unsweetened chocolate in the top of a double boiler set over simmering water, stirring until smooth. Remove from over the water and let cool for 10 minutes.

Sift the flour, baking soda, and salt into a medium-sized bowl. Beat the brown sugar and butter together in a large bowl until blended. Add the egg; beat well. Beat in the yolk. Add the melted chocolate and beat until blended. Mix in the dry ingredients alternately with the buttermilk, beginning and ending with dry ingredients. Add the boiling water and vanilla, stirring until blended (the batter will be thin).

Pour the batter into your prepared pan. Bake until a tester inserted into center comes out clean, about 35 minutes. Transfer the pan to a rack and cool completely. *(The cake can be prepared 1 day ahead. Cover with foil and store at room temperature.)*

Beat the cream in a large bowl until stiff peaks form. Spoon 1½ cups of whipped cream into the bottom of large glass trifle bowl. Sprinkle with ½ cup of toffee bits. Crumble one-third of the cake over the toffee. Continue layering whipped cream, toffee bits, and cake, creating three layers of each. Spoon the remaining whipped cream over top, spreading to cover. Cover the trifle and refrigerate for at least 4 hours. *(The trifle can be prepared 1 day ahead. Keep refrigerated.)*

Sprinkle with chocolate shavings and serve.

Cycle Santa

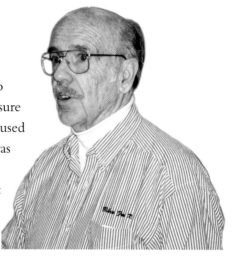

When Chuck Graeb was growing up in the Bronx, there was one thing he always wanted, but his family could never afford: a bike. So about a dozen years ago, when Chuck retired, he decided to make sure no other kid went without a bicycle. "I thought I would get a few used bikes, fix them up, and give them away to needy kids," he says, "I was thinking maybe a dozen or so at Christmastime."

Chuck got his neighbor involved, but the first two years didn't go too well. "I guess people didn't trust us," he says. "They would say, 'What are you gonna do with the bikes—sell them?' We got a lot of that."

Chuck's neighbor gave up on the plan, but Chuck said, "I'm gonna give it one more year." That year the project "exploded," to use his word. People donated about seventy-five used bikes, and every year since then the number has grown. Chuck now gives away about five hundred bikes a year. Most come from parents whose children have outgrown them. Some are from police departments, which hold stolen bikes for a year to see if they're claimed. Wal-Mart donates bikes that are a little scratched or dented.

"I guess I'm like a glorified garbage man," Chuck laughs. "It costs me about thirty-five dollars to fix each bike, so I have to screen the bikes, because if they need too much work, it's not worth it."

Of course he can't repair all those bikes by himself, so Chuck enlisted shop classes from every high school from Old Saybrook to Branford to help. Now he's signing up helpers in Middletown and Hartford.

Recently Chuck started giving away bikes to foster children, too. "One came up to me who was about eight years old and had lived in a lot of places. He said to me, 'Nobody wants me.' That broke my heart, and I thought, at least these kids should have something to call their own. It shows them that somebody out there cares for them."

At Chuck's Christmas bike giveaway parties, the kids are on one side of the room and the bikes lined up on the other. When Chuck says, "Go!" the kids, shrieking and laughing, run to claim the bike they want. "It's absolute madness," he says, and "wonderful."

Lighthouse Santa

The days when the lonely lighthouse keeper was isolated in his watery outpost are over, but in New England a joyful holiday tradition abides. Flying Santa still visits the lighthouses, bringing gifts to those who tend them. Since the late 1920s volunteers dressed as Santa have boarded a plane or helicopter to travel a special route up and down the Atlantic seashore.

It started in early December in 1929, when floatplane pilot William Wincapaw encountered a storm just off the Maine coast. He followed the beacons from the lighthouses and managed to get home safely. To show his appreciation, he made a return trip over the lighthouses on Christmas Day, dropping small gifts to the keepers he believed had saved his life. The gifts were so warmly received that a tradition was born and continued without a break until World War II. Local companies helped out, donating coffee, candy, and small luxuries for the men and their wives, along with toys for their children. With the war's end in 1945, the flights resumed and expanded to include lighthouses from southern New England to the Canadian border.

In the late 1940s maritime historian and adventurer Edward Rowe Snow took over as the aerial St. Nick, sometimes losing his fake whiskers as he leaned out the window for a package drop. Over the years, fewer and fewer lighthouses were staffed; still, Snow felt that the Coast Guard personnel and civilians who maintained them should be thanked. He added Coast Guard boat stations, too.

These days twenty-two working lights remain on Long Island Sound, and Chief Warrant Officer John Strauser is the Coast Guard officer in charge of all of them. The only staffed

Stratford Point Lighthouse.

lighthouse left in the United States is in Boston, but the Stratford Point Lighthouse comes pretty close. Since the signal is automated, Officer Strauser is technically not the lighthouse keeper, but he and his family live at Stratford Point, a place that John and his wife truly love.

"It's a peaceful place to live," says Officer Strauser, who enjoys walking the rocky beach. Although the lighthouse is not officially open to the public, it attracts quite a few visitors. John welcomes them, taking them inside the tower, explaining the light's history, and showing off the magnificent lamp with its Fresnel lens that guided ships for a hundred years.

John thinks he knows why people are drawn to lighthouses. "Lighthouses have always been a symbol of faith," he says, "a symbol of safe haven. They find it very comforting to see a lighthouse."

On a December afternoon, John and several other Coast Guardsmen are gathered with their families outside Stratford Point Light as St. Nick, using a Bell Jet Ranger helicopter for a sleigh, lightly touches down beside the red-and-white lighthouse.

George Morgan, the Flying Santa since 1982, can stay for just a few minutes. His day is a whirlwind of more than a dozen stops, taking in Lynde Point Light in Old Saybrook and Stratford Point Light. With his white hair and beard, George really looks the part of the jolly old elf. He's been making the flights since the Hull Lifesaving Museum took responsibility for Flying Santa. The Friends of Flying Santa, a volunteer group, raises money to keep the program going. "I'm seventy years old," George declares, "I'm getting too old for this!" But his smile widens as he hands packages to the kids, and it's easy to believe he'd have a hard time giving this up. After a few jolly laughs and a couple of smart salutes, Flying Santa takes off to continue spreading cheer along the coast. For the Strausers and the other Coast Guard families, the visit is a sign that their service is remembered, and cherished.

Church bells peal on Christmas day. Clockwise from top left: Redding Center, Sherman, Monroe, Washington, Plymouth, Cornwall Bridge, Middlebury, Woodbridge, Branford (center).

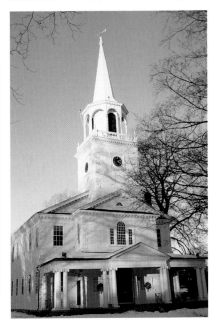

"Nguzo Saba—can you say that?" Kerry Cole asks the third-graders. "En-goo-zoo-sah-bah," the children repeat.

"Those are the seven guiding principles of Kwanzaa, which is the festival of the first fruits of the harvest," Kerry explains.

Inside a small store called Dygnyti Books on Dixwell Avenue in Hamden, a new holiday tradition is taking root. Kerry Cole is teaching New Haven schoolchildren about Kwanzaa. "It's not a religious holiday. Some people might think Kwanzaa is replacing Christmas but it isn't," she tells them.

Celebration, *a Kwanzaa quilt by artist Ed Johnetta Miller of Hartford.*

Kwanzaa began a little more than thirty years ago as a way for African Americans to celebrate their past and learn about African history and customs. About fifteen million people worldwide now celebrate it.

On a small table spread with an African-print cloth, Kerry has set up a *kinara*—a candleholder with seven candles in it, one black, three red, and three green. The kinara sits atop a *mkeka*, a place mat made of straw. Spread alongside the kinara is *mazao*, or crops, including small pumpkins and ears of corn.

Kerry raises a wooden goblet called a *kikombe cha umoja* or communal unity cup and begins the libation ceremony. Pouring water from the cup in the direction of the four winds, she recites these words:

> *For the Motherland cradle of civilization.*
> *For the ancestors and their indomitable spirit.*
> *For the elders from whom we can learn much.*
> *For our youth who represent the promise for tomorrow.*
> *For our people, the original people.*
> *For our struggle and in remembrance of those who have struggled on our behalf.*
> *For Umoja the principle of unity, which should guide us in all that we do.*
> *For the creator who provides all things great and small.*

For seven nights starting on December 26 a candle is lit in a kinara. Each candle represents a principle for daily living, ranging from *imani*, or faith, to unity, *umoja*. The words come from the African language Swahili.

Poetry, dance, song, and drumming were part of the Kwanzaa event held at the Long Wharf Theater in New Haven.

"Can you guys say *umoja*?" Kerry asks. The children repeat after her as she explains, "That means 'unity,' and we should strive to maintain unity in the family, in the community, in the nation, and in the race."

Lily Perkins, a New Haven teacher, says the principles should be applied year-round. "These principles could be adapted to all of our lifestyles, and I would like to see that happen. Unity, determination, economic cooperation; it's important to embrace those principles as human beings."

Handmade gifts known as *zawadi* are exchanged as a reward for commitments made and kept during the year. Kerry says the gifts are meant as symbols. "It's all about family and it's all about celebrating and it's not about how much I can give you or how much I can get from you. It's about love. It's about unity and it's about black people who are redefining themselves, coming back into themselves, remembering themselves and remembering their past."

If your family is thinking of celebrating Kwanzaa, there are a lot of books out there to help you initiate the customs, crafts, and cooking. Kerry recommends *Kwanzaa: A Celebration of Family Community and Culture,* written by the founder of the holiday, Maulana Karenga.

For many families, Kwanzaa is a new holiday tradition. It can be celebrated each night of Kwanzaa at Dygnyti Books in Hamden, where Kerry holds a program for the public. She also goes to schools to teach Kwanzaa programs. In Norwalk, the Norwalk Museum sponsors a Kwanzaa celebration each year, which is produced by local residents and merchants. Drumming and dancing and activities for children are featured, along with music, an art exhibit, and vendors selling African-American merchandise, including kinara and other items needed to celebrate the holiday. Other Kwanzaa celebrations are organized by the Stepping Stones Museum for Children in Norwalk and the Amistad Foundation of the Hartford Atheneum.

Three Kings

On January 6, twelve days after Christmas, Latinos celebrate Three Kings Day. Known in other cultures as the Epiphany, "Dia de los Tres Reyes Magos" commemorates the Biblical story of the wisemen who followed the Star of Bethlehem to worship the newborn Christ child and to bring Him gifts of gold, frankincense, and myrrh. The night before Three Kings Day, Latino children traditionally leave hay in their shoes for the camels ridden by the kings. In the morning they find their shoes filled with gifts and treats.

In Hartford the holiday is celebrated with a parade featuring the Magi riding proudly through the streets on camels and paso fino horses. The parade ends at the Pope Park Recreation Center, where children enjoy a party and presents—delivered by the kings!

One of Connecticut's newest children's museums, Stepping Stones in Norwalk, celebrates Three Kings Day several times during the month of December. Kids are invited to decorate crowns and wear them in a parade around the museum.

Candlelight Caroling at Lourdes

Though most of the people who make the pilgrimage to Lourdes in Litchfield come when the leaves on the trees form a canopy over this church without walls, the shrine is open year-round. The annual Christmas Festival draws the faithful, despite the wintry weather. Thirty thousand a year flock here to pray at the stone grotto, which resembles the Grotto of Our Lady of Lourdes in France, where Catholics believe the Virgin Mary appeared to a girl named Bernadette.

Father Eugene Lynch studied for the priesthood in Litchfield before the Montfort Missionaries, a community of brothers and priests, built the shrine. He remembers the site as a rocky ledge with a babbling stream. Then in 1954 two of the brothers from the Montfort community in Italy arrived. "They operated a farm to feed these hungry seminarians, and in their spare time they started building the shrine," says Father Lynch.

Four years later the shrine grotto was completed and dedicated. From May through mid-October chipmunks scamper across the stones as the three resident priests celebrate Mass or anoint the sick.

Colette Boyd visits often and calls it an "awesome experience." She says of the open-air church, "You feel like you're with God and you're in His creation." Others meditate as they climb a quarter-mile-long trail through the woods that leads them through the Stations of the Cross, depicting the sufferings and death of Christ in bronze figures. People who visit say they feel a holy presence here, and never more so than at Christmas, when they gather to celebrate Christ's birth.

Carolers clutching candles are led to the grotto by the glow of five hundred luminaria lining the walkway. Candlelight caroling is one of three highlights of the annual Christmas Festival Weekend at the shrine. On Saturday morning families work together constructing gingerbread nativity scenes. The caroling takes place Saturday evening. On Sunday afternoon more than a hundred children from several community churches stage a living nativity, complete with livestock. As visitors stroll the long walkway through the property, they are greeted by characters from the Christmas pageant, who share a spiritual message with them.

Donna Valente speaks for many visitors when she says, "This place has always been very special. It's a feeling of peace and it's an almost overwhelming feeling of beauty."

For those who visit in December, Lourdes of Litchfield is a peaceful place to meditate on the meaning of Christmas.

The Toyman

Walking unobtrusively through the hallways of Bridgeport Hospital, Eric Hultgren doesn't look much like Santa Claus. His sport coat and slacks are a long way from a red velvet suit, and there's no sack of toys slung over his shoulder. Eric's handmade wooden toys are tucked neatly into a shopping bag. But when the sick children on the pediatric floor see him, they *know*. You can see it in their smiles, and in his.

The toys were Eric's wife's idea, something Shirley cooked up to keep Eric's mind off her battle with lung cancer. Eric figured making the toys was his end of a bargain with God. "I thought, *I'm gonna do something to help other people and maybe the Lord will help us.* But," he sighs ruefully, "it didn't work out."

Or maybe that prayer was answered in an unexpected way. Although Shirley died, the toymaking she inspired helped Eric go on living. He had a reason to get well after quintuple-bypass surgery and a bout with prostate cancer. He kept on going because of the kids, and the toys.

Eric started with cars and trucks. He later invented toys specifically for children confined to a hospital bed, like a fishing pole with a wooden fish dangling at the end of the line.

When I reported on Eric one year it unleashed a flood of national media attention. That led to truckloads of fan mail—more than eight thousand letters. Some contained money to buy

materials for toys. But Eric's pension and Social Security were enough to cover that. "If I were to take the money for it, then I would lose the kick of giving it away."

Instead Eric saved the contributions to use as seed money. He got together with the Bridgeport Hospital Foundation to publish a letter about his toys and the joy they've brought to children in the hospital. Then they mailed one to all the people who'd written to him, appealing to them to help Eric raise money to improve the children's floor at the hospital.

"We can do better for the kids," he said. "It's kind of dingy here, and there's not much room for them to play or for mom or dad to sleep over."

That dream carried Eric through another bad time, another bout with cancer. With his help the foundation ultimately raised $1.5 million to refurbish the children's floor, turning it into a cheery place with a circus theme and a playroom shaped like a circus big top.

"I'm eighty-one now, and I guess I am slowing down," Eric says, though it would be hard to figure how. He's still making toys, dropping off his last batch at the hospital right before Christmas. He's even branched out into some new creations, like Mr. Toad's car, inspired by *The Wind in the Willows*.

And he's planning another letter campaign to organize new groups all over the nation to use his diagrams to make toys for hospitalized children.

"It's a great life," Eric likes to say, and it is, because Eric Hultgren is bringing happiness to children, and he keeps the spirit of the season alive all year.

Cards That Care

Christmas cards are a traditional way of spreading holiday cheer, but when buying the cards can make a difference in someone's life, they are even more special. *The Kennedy Center of Bridgeport* celebrated its fiftieth anniversary in 2001, and each year it helps more than a thousand people who have psychiatric disabilities, traumatic brain injuries, mental retardation, and learning and physical disabilities. The art therapy programs in Milford and Bridgeport let Kennedy Center artists transcend their disabilities by expressing themselves through painting and drawing. Each year some of these artworks are chosen to become greeting cards. Buying the cards may mean a child with spina bifida will have swimming lessons, or a young adult with mental retardation will learn the money management skills he needs to hold a job and live independently. Cards and envelopes can be personalized with a company or family name.

   The Greater Hartford Association for Retarded Citizens has as its mission "changing the lives of those who have mental retardation, and the minds of those who don't." HARC, as the agency is known, has been doing just that for fifty years. HARC was founded by parents of people with mental retardation to ensure that their children would enjoy "health, happiness, independence, a good job and enduring relationships"—in other words, the kind of life we all want to live. HARC provides an array of programs, including The ArtSparks Group. Artists exhibit their work in area galleries, and have recently branched out into creating holiday cards. The entire proceeds from the cards go into the Client Assistance Fund.

Winter Wonder *by Todd Carboni (above), one of the cards offered by the Kennedy Center. Left: Original watercolor collage by The ArtSparks Group of HARC.*

Frosty and friends, clockwise from top left: Wilton, Chester, New Haven, Milford, Westport, Chester.

Resources

Feeling Festive

Connecticut's First Christmas Tree, page 3: Noden-Reed Park Museum, 58 West Street, Windsor Locks. The museum holds Victorian Christmas Open House Days annually. A Noden-Reed stamp is available to stamp holiday greeting cards. (860) 627–9212.

A Victorian Tree Extravaganza, page 4: Lockwood-Mathews Mansion Museum, 295 West Avenue, Norwalk. The Victorian Holiday exhibition in early December usually includes special events for families. (203) 838–9799; www.lockwoodmathews.org.

Atheneum Festival of Trees and Traditions, page 7: Held at the Wadsworth Atheneum, 600 Main Street, downtown Hartford. The festival kicks off with a preview party the second Friday after Thanksgiving and opens to the public the next day. (860) 278–2670, extension 3034; www.wadsworthfestival.org.

Christmas Impressions, page 8: The Florence Griswold Museum, 96 Lyme Street, Old Lyme. A lengthy program of holiday events and workshops ranges from a teddy bear tea and story hour for children to classes in such things as making traditional holiday kissing balls. (860) 434–5542; www.flogris.org.

The Fairfield Christmas Tree Festival, page 11: The three-day festival held at the Burr Homestead on Old Post Road in Fairfield includes a gala on the first Thursday evening after Thanksgiving, a children's event on Friday, and other events. Tickets are required for the children's event, and they sell out quickly. For advance tickets or information, write to the Fairfield Christmas Tree Festival, P.O. Box 844, Southport, CT 06490.

A Capitol Idea, page 12: For information about the Bushnell Park event, call the Greater Hartford Arts Council at (860) 525–8629 or visit www.connectthedots.org.

More Capital Lights, page 13: The Hartford Festival of Light is held on Constitution Plaza in downtown Hartford from the day after Thanksgiving until Three Kings Day in January.

Holiday Glow, page 15: *Hubbard Park,* 1 Cahill Avenue, off West Main Street, 7/10 mile from I–691. Lighted from late November through early January; admission is free. Call the Department of Parks and Recreation at (203) 630–4259. *UI Fantasy of Lights* in New Haven's Lighthouse Park opens mid-November and runs through New Year's Eve. Open 5:00 to 9:00 P.M. Sunday through Thursday, 5:00 to 10:00 P.M. Friday and Saturday. Admission fee per vehicle or buses; per-car charge slightly higher on Saturday and Sunday. All proceeds go to Easter Seals Goodwill Industries for programs that help people with disabilities. Call (203) 777–2000. Located in Beardsley Park in Bridgeport, *Park City Lights* opens after Thanksgiving and runs through the first week in January. Admission charged according to vehicle size. Call (203) 576–7016. The Hartford *Holiday Light Fantasia* lights up Goodwin Park on the Hartford-Wethersfield line. Starts the night before Thanksgiving and runs through Three King's Day in January. Open Sunday through Thursday 5:00 to 10:00 P.M., Friday and Saturday 5:00 to 11:00 P.M. Per-car admission fee. A portion of the proceeds goes to the Connecticut Children's Medical Center. Call (860) 723–6184.

O Little Town, page 17: The Bethlehem Post Office, 34 East Street, Bethlehem 06751. The lobby's holiday hours for cachet and mailing cards are Monday through Friday 6:30 A.M. to 5:30 P.M., Saturday 6:30 A.M. to 4:00 P.M., and Sunday noon to 4:00 P.M. When sending cards to be canceled with the Bethlehem postmark, address the package to Joan Manzi, Postmaster.

The Bethlehem Festival, page 18: Bethlehem Christmas Town Festival is held the first week in December. Admission is free, and free shuttle buses transport visitors from the parking area at the fairgrounds on Route 61. (203) 266–5557; www.ci.bethlehem.ct.us.

Come to the Manger, page 21: Abbey of Regina Laudis, 273 Flanders Road, Bethlehem. Terce and Mass are celebrated daily at 7:50 A.M. Vespers is sung at 5:00 P.M., 4:30 P.M. on Sundays. The church, chapel, art shop, and crèche are open to the public. www.abbeyofreginalaudis.com.

Christmas by Lantern Light, page 24: Mystic Seaport Christmas Lantern Light Tour tickets go on sale at the end of September for Seaport members, in October for the general public. Tours held from the beginning through the middle of December. Weekend tours sell out quickly. For reservations, call (888) 9–SEAPORT.

Make a Joyful Noise

Poetry and Prayer, page 30: The Alliance Theater is a resident theater company of the University of New Haven. The Black Nativity is performed on the second and third weekends of December at the Dodds Hall Theatre on the university campus at 300 Orange Avenue, West Haven. (203) 932–7085.

Live Nativities, page 33: For information on the Valley Brook Community Church's live nativity in Granby, call Pastor Clark Pfaff at (860) 844–0001.

Trees in the Rigging, page 34: Held in Essex the Sunday after Thanksgiving. Call the Connecticut River Museum at (860) 767–8269 or visit www.essexct.com.

Christmas City of Connecticut, page 35: Norwich Winter Festival begins the day after Thanksgiving. The festival parade is held the afternoon of the second Saturday after Thanksgiving.

Holiday on Parade, page 37: The *Old Saybrook Christmas Torchlight Parade and Muster* takes place the second Saturday in December at 6:00 P.M., regardless of weather. *Groton White Lights Holiday Parade* takes place at 5:00 P.M. the second Saturday in December. For information contact Groton Utilities at (860) 446–4000. The *Montville Holiday Light Parade* heads down Route 32 through town at dusk on the first Sunday in December. The *Niantic Light Parade* heads down Main Street just after dark on the second Sunday in December. Wallingford's *Season of Celebrations* is held in the historic town center all day long on the first Saturday in December. (203) 284–1807.

Siggy Sings, page 39: The Saybrook Stroll is held on Main Street in Old Saybrook the first Friday night in December.

Standing Ovation, page 40: The Hartford Chorale and Hartford Symphony Orchestra perform *Messiah* in early December at the Bushnell Center for the Performing Arts. Call the Bushnell box office at (860) 987–5900, visit the chorale's Web site at www.hartfordchorale.org, or visit the orchestra's Web site at www.hartfordsymphony.org.

The Colonial Concert, page 41: Orchestra New England's Colonial Concert is usually scheduled for the last weekend in November. It sells out, so buy tickets early. (203) 934–8863; www.orchestranewengland.org.

Holiday Performances, page 42: Santa Lucia Festival is held the first Friday in December at Emanuel Lutheran Church, 311 Capitol Avenue, Hartford; (860) 525–0894. Make We Joy is held the first Sunday in December at Harkness Chapel, Connecticut College, New London; (860) 439–2450. Annual tuba concert dates vary each year; call the Valley Railroad Company in Essex at (860) 767–0103.

Sights and Sounds of Christmas, page 43: Sights and Sounds of Christmas is held at the Black Rock Congregational Church, 3685 Black Rock Turnpike, Fairfield, CT 06432. Admission is a contribution of nonperishable food. Tickets required. (203) 255–7664.

Symphony on Ice, page 44: United Technologies Symphony on Ice is held at the Hartford Civic Center in early December. For tickets, contact public libraries in the greater Hartford area.

The Nutcracker, page 45: For information about the Hartford-based Dance Connecticut troupe, call (860) 525–9396. Elsewhere in the state, other performances of *The Nutcracker* are held at The Warner Theater, Torrington; Charles Ives Center, Danbury; Palace Theater, Stamford; and the Shubert Theater, New Haven.

Songs of Joy, page 46: The Chorus Angelicus *Christmas Angelicus* CD is available through Pelagos Music, Inc., in Norfolk. (877) 735–2467; www.pelagosmusic.com. Copies of the Trinity Choir of Men and Boys CD *Christmas Around* are available through the music office at Trinity Episcopal Church on the Green in New Haven. (203) 776–2616; www.trinitynewhaven.org.

Twelfth Night, page 48: The Boar's Head Festival is held at the Asylum Hill Congregational Church at 814 Asylum Avenue in Hartford. (860) 525–5696; www.ahcc.org.

Deck the Halls

Mr. Whipple's Wonderland, page 52: Pineville Road in the Dayville section of Killingly. Opens right after Thanksgiving and remains open through New Year's Day, 5:00 to 9:00 each evening. (860) 774–2742.

All Decked Out, page 56: Lexington Road near Walnut Hill Park, across the street from the New Britain Museum of American Art. Hours are advertised in the *New Britain Herald,* but generally the house is open to the public December 21, 22, and 23 from 6:00 to 9:00 P.M., with daytime hours for school field trips.

Home for the Holidays, page 59: The Hartford House Tour benefiting the Mark Twain House generally takes place on a Sunday early in December. Tickets are required and include refreshments in the carriage house at the Mark Twain House, 351 Farmington Avenue, Hartford. (860) 247–0998; www.marktwainhouse.org. For information about the Cheshire house tour, contact the Church of the

Epiphany at (203) 272–4355. For information about the Westport Historical Society holiday tour, call (203) 222–1424. For information about the Holiday House Tour in Granby, contact the Salmon Brook Historical Society at (860) 653–9713; www.salmonbrookhistorical.org.

Christmas Past, page 62: The Milford Historical Society Holiday House Tour takes place in early December in even-numbered years. Candlelight and daylight tours are available. (203) 874–2664; http://sites.netscape.net/milfordhistoric/index.html.

The Pleasure of Your Company, page 65: Hill-Stead Museum, 36 Mountain Road, Farmington. (860) 677–4787; www.hillstead.org.

More Historical Holidays in Farmington, page 66: Stanley-Whitman House, 37 High Street, Farmington. (860) 677–9222.

Christmas with the First Family, page 68: The governor's residence is located at 990 Prospect Avenue in Hartford, at the corner of Asylum Avenue. The annual Holiday Open House Tour begins the Wednesday after Thanksgiving. The governor and first lady greet the crowds on the first morning from 10:00 A.M. to noon. Tours continue Thursday through Saturday 10:00 A.M. to 3:00 P.M. and Sunday noon to 3:00 P.M. Admission is one new, unwrapped toy to be given to a needy child. (860) 566–4840.

Heart and Hand

Christmas in the Mansion, page 74: Christmas in the Mansion, Lauralton Hall, 200 High Street, Milford. Open for three days, generally the first weekend in December. Admission charge for adults. (203) 877–2786.

Noel Boutique, page 75: The three-day event held at St. Maurice's parish hall, Wightman Road, New Britain, is open the first Thursday, Friday, and Saturday of November. For information write to the Junior League of Greater New Britain, P.O. Box 2525, New Britain, CT 06050. (860) 223–2231.

Made in Connecticut, page 76: Howland Hughes Department Store, 120–140 Bank Street, Waterbury. (800) 474–6728; www.theconnecticutstore.com.

Goodies from Home, page 77: The Connecticut Creative Store is located at the Department of Agriculture at 765 Asylum Avenue in Hartford, directly across from the Hartford Insurance Company. Free parking behind the building. Open 11:00 A.M. to 2:00 P.M. Monday through Friday. For information or to place an order, contact the Connecticut Department of Agriculture at (860) 713–2503; www.state.ct.us/doag.

Handmade Holiday, page 78: For information write to A Trail of Connecticut Craft Centers, P.O. Box 1113, Simsbury, CT 06070, or call (888) CT–CRAFT. The shop at *Guilford Handcraft Center* is just off I–95 exit 58 and is open seven days a week. The holiday sale generally begins early in November and lasts through Christmas Eve. (203) 453–5947; www.handcraftcenter.org. *Wesleyan Potters,* 350 South Main Street, Middletown. (860) 347–5925; www.wesleyanpotters.com. *Farmington Valley Arts Center,* 25 Arts Center Lane, Avon Park North, Avon. (860) 678–1867. *Brookfield Craft Center* is on Route 25 just east of the intersection with U.S. Routes 7 and 202. (203) 775–4526; www.brookfieldcraftcenter.org. *Creative Arts Workshop,* 80 Audubon Street, New Haven. A parking garage is next to the center. (203) 562–4927.

Paper Dolls, page 81: Write to Patti Kierys, P.O. Box 603, New Hartford, CT 06057.

Gifts from the Sea, page 82: John Wilson's ornaments are sold in shops from Connecticut to Maine. Locally you'll find them at the Silver Skate in Niantic (860–739–8913) and the Sand Castle at Bittersweet Farm in Branford (203–481–9392).

Crafted in Connecticut, page 83: Susan Miller-Ceskavich's Jingle Balls are available at Wojtusiks Christmas Shop, Route 6, Bristol; Diana Mihaltse, Whimsies and Folk Art on Tin, 24 Overidge Lane, Wilton, (203) 762–7765; Primrose Path ornaments, 2278 Main Street, Stratford, (203) 375–2006; Hepburn Glass Ornaments, Killingworth, (860) 663–1169.

A Living Doll House, page 84: For information on Louis Nichole dolls, ornaments, and home furnishings, visit www.louisnichole.com. Ornaments are sold in Connecticut at Lexington Gardens in Newtown (203–426–3161), Favorite Things in Durham (860–349–8063), Century Florists & Gifts in Rocky Hill (860–563–5084), and Windover Garden & Florist in Bethlehem (203–266–7010).

Mattatuck Festival of the Trees, page 86: Mattatuck Museum, 144 West Main Street, Waterbury. The annual tree festival is held for ten days. (203) 753–0381.

Visions of Sugarplums

The Santa Special, page 92: The Santa Special and other Essex Steam Train holiday excursions start after Thanksgiving and run until Christmas Eve. For schedules and ticket information contact The Valley Railroad Company, One Railroad Avenue, P.O. Box 452, Essex, CT 06426; (860) 767–0103 or (800) 377–3987; www.essexsteamtrain.com.

The Holiday Express, page 94: The Danbury Railway Museum, 120 White Street, Danbury. (203) 778–8337; www.danbury.org/org/drm.

More Holiday Trains and Trolleys, page 95: *Railroad Museum of New England* is just off East Main Street in Thomaston. (860) 283–RAIL; www.rmne.org. *Connecticut Trolley Museum,* 58 North Road, East Windsor. (860) 627–6540; www.ceraonline.org. *Shore Line Trolley Museum,* 17 River Street, East Haven. (203) 467–6927; www.bera.org.

The Man Who Saved Christmas, page 96: Eli Whitney Museum, 915 Whitney Avenue, Hamden. (203) 777–1833; www.eliwhitney.org.

Christmas Village, page 99: Christmas Village is located at the upper end of Church Street in Torrington. Open early December through Christmas Eve, 1:00 to 8:30 P.M. every day, except Christmas Eve, when the

hours are earlier. Admission is free; complimentary hot chocolate when lines are long. For information call the Torrington Recreation Department at (860) 489–2274.

Playthings of the Past, page 101: The Wilton Heritage Museum *Playthings of the Past* exhibit is open December and January at the Betts-Sturges-Blackmar House. (203) 762–7257.

Chocolate Lace, page 102: For the names of local retail outlets, call (203) 792–1234.

The Chocolate Factory, page 103: Thompson Candy is sold in stores nationwide. The factory outlet store at 80 Vine Street in Meriden is open 9:00 A.M. to 5:00 P.M. Monday through Saturday. (203) 235–2541.

Tasty Town, page 106: Gingerbread Village is on view at St. George's Episcopal Church on Tucker Hill Road in Middlebury for one week beginning the first Saturday in December. (203) 758–9864.

Winter Wonderland

All Spruced Up, page 112: Wrights Mill Farm, 63 Creasey Road, Canterbury. (860) 774–1455; www.wrightsmillfarm.com. The Jones Family Farms, 266 Israel Hill Road, Shelton. (203) 929–8425; www.jonesfamilyfarms.com.

More Christmas Trees, page 114: To learn about tree farms across the state, call the Connecticut Christmas Tree Growers Association at (860) 376–2370 or visit www.ctchristmastree.org. Tree and shrub seedlings are available from the Connecticut State Nursery for Connecticut landowners. Call (860) 376–2513 or write to DEP Division of Forestry, Connecticut State Nursery, 190 Sheldon Road, Voluntown, CT 06384.

A Passion for Poinsettias, page 115: University of Connecticut Greenhouse, Storrs Road, Storrs. The public is always welcome at the greenhouse, and open houses are held occasionally. (860) 486–2042.

Dashing through the Snow, page 121: Allegra Farm and the Horse Drawn Carriage and Sleigh Museum of New England, Route 82, East Haddam. Private or shared sleigh rides available. The museum is open Saturday and Sunday 11:00 A.M. to 5:00 P.M.; weekdays and groups by reservation. Call ahead for winter hours and events. (860) 873–9658; www.allegrafarm.com.

Sleigh Bells Ring, page 123: Bevin Brothers Manufacturing Company, P.O. Box 60, East Hampton, CT 06424; (860) 267–4431.

Ahead of Her Time, page 124: The Kellogg Environmental Center and Osborne Homestead Museum, 500 Hawthorne Avenue, Derby. (203) 734–2513; (203) 922–7832.

A Fine Feathered Christmas, page 127: To get involved in a Christmas bird count, call the Audubon Society at (203) 264–5098 or visit www.audubon.org or www.ctbirding.org. Local chapters of the Connecticut Audubon Society hold other seasonal events, including holiday boutiques with nature-related gifts. The Connecticut Audubon Center in Fairfield also operates a Christmas tree farm at the H. Smith Richardson Sanctuary at Sasco Creek Road in Westport.

Reindeer Games, page 129: Beardsley Zoological Gardens, 1875 Noble Avenue, Bridgeport. The zoo is open from 9:00 A.M. to 4:00 P.M. daily; closes early on Christmas Eve and New Year's Eve; closed Christmas and New Year's Days. Admission charged. If you visit during the holiday season, please bring a nonperishable food item or pet food to donate to the Beardsley Zoo's collection for area food banks and animal shelters. (203) 394–6565; www.beardsleyzoo.org.

Spirit of the Season

A Cup of Christmas Tea, page 132: For information about the Norma T. Pfriem Cancer Center, call (203) 384–8000.

Royal Trifle, page 133: Recipe courtesy of the Royal Tea Company, Trumbull; (203) 452–1006.

Cycle Santa, page 134: To donate a bike or make a financial contribution to Chuck Graeb's Bikes for Kids, call (860) 434–3684.

Lighthouse Santa, page 135: For more on the history of Santa's flights, or to make a donation, contact Friends of Flying Santa Inc., P.O. Box 791, Hull, MA 02045-0791; (781) 925–0783; www.flyingsanta.com.

Keeping Kwanzaa, page 138: Each night of Kwanzaa, Kerry Cole of Dygnyti Books on Dixwell Avenue in Hamden holds a program for the public; Kerry also goes to schools to teach Kwanzaa programs.

(203) 776–9061. The Norwalk Museum sponsors a Kwanzaa celebration each year. (203) 866–0202. For information about Ed Johnetta Miller quilts, contact her at 20 Plainfield Street, Hartford, CT 06112; (860) 727–8552; edquilt@aol.com.

Three Kings, page 140: For information about the Hartford Three Kings festivities, contact the Spanish American Merchants' Association at (860) 278–5825. Stepping Stones Museum (303 West Avenue, Norwalk) reaches out to a diverse population of kids age one through ten, with celebrations of Kwanzaa, Hanukkah, Christmas, Ramadan, Diwali, and the Feast of Santa Lucia. (203) 899–0606; www.steppingstonesmuseum.org.

Candlelight Caroling at Lourdes, page 141: The Christmas Festival at Lourdes generally occurs the weekend before Christmas. Call ahead to make reservations—some people call as early as October. For more information write to the Reverend Father Director, Lourdes in Litchfield, P.O. Box 667, Litchfield, CT 06759. (860) 567–7434; www.montfortmissionaries.com/lourdes/phtml.

The Toyman, page 142: To make a donation, contact the Bridgeport Hospital Foundation, 267 Grant Street, P.O. Box 5000, Bridgeport, CT 06610; (203) 384–3522.

Cards That Care, page 143: To order cards, contact Kennedy Center Card Department, 184 Garden Street, Bridgeport, CT 06605; (203) 332–4535. Or contact the Greater Hartford Association for Retarded Citizens, Inc. to order ArtSparks cards: HARC, 900 Asylum Avenue, Hartford CT 06105-1985; (860) 278–1100, extension 247.

Comstock covered bridge, Colchester.

Photo Credits

Many thanks to the following people and organizations for providing photographs and pictures:

Allegra Farm: 121, photo by Ernie Larsen 122

Beardsley Zoological Garden: 129

Black Rock Congregational Church: 43

Bridgeport Hospital, photo by D. Ottenstein: 142

Paula Brisco: 98 (top left)

Les Burdge Photography: 126, 127 (all except bottom left), 128 (top right, center left)

Central Connecticut Tourism District: 119 (second row left and bottom right)

Coastal Fairfield Convention and Visitors Bureau, photo by Stuart Smith: 19

Connecticut College, photos by William Mercer (top left and bottom right), photo by Tim Martin (center left): 42

Connecticut's Mystic and More! Convention and Visitors Bureau, www.mysticmore.com, photos by Michael Melford: 8, 67 (center left), 152

Creative Arts Workshop: 79 (top left), 79 (center and bottom, photos by Harold Shapiro)

Cuprak Family: 36

Dance Connecticut: 45

Nancy Freeborn: 73, 81–82, 83 (all but bottom right), 89 (bottom right), 102, 103 (bottom left), 104, 134

Greater Hartford Arts Council, photo by Lori Kupec: 13

The Greater Hartford Association for Retarded Citizens, Inc.: 143 (left)

Guilford Handcraft Center, Inc.: 78

Hartford Chorale, Thomas Giroir Photography: 40

Howland Hughes Department Store: 76

Joyful Noise, Inc., photo by Joan Walden: 46

Kennedy Center of Bridgeport: 143 (right)

Patti Kierys: 72

Teresa Layman: 108

Litchfield Hills Travel Council, photos by Janet L. Serra: 118, 137 (bottom center)

Louis Nichole, Inc., photos by Feliciano Garcia: 84–85

Mattatuck Museum, photos by Bill O. Cotner: 86

McConnell & McNamara: i, iii, 14 (except bottom right), 27 (bottom right), 117 (top left, bottom left), 119 (second row right, third row right)

Ed Johnetta Miller: 138

Mystic Seaport: 24–26

Norwich Bulletin, photo by Jeff Evans: 35

Kelly Quinlan, Shore Line Newspapers: 39

Lisa Reneson: ii, 18, 22, 67 (center right), 69 (bottom), 70, 87 (center), 89 (bottom center), 93 (top), 95 (top left and right), 99–100, 103 (lower right), 109, 117 (center left), 125

Ronald Robinson: 1, 7, 9–10, 12, 14 (bottom right), 15–16, 19 (all except bottom center), 20, 37, 38 (top left and right), 42 (top right, center right, bottom left), 48–59, 60 (top), 62, 64, 67 (upper center, upper right, center, bottom left), 68, 69 (top), 71 (all but upper left, second row left), 74 (bottom), 75 (top), 80, 83 (bottom right), 87 (upper right, center right), 89 (upper left and right, center left, center), 90, 92, 93 (bottom), 94, 95 (bottom), 97, 98 (top right), 105–7, 110–14, 117 (top right), 119 (top right, third row left and center, bottom left), 124, 128 (center, bottom left and right), 130–31, 137 (all except bottom center), 144 (top left and right, center right), 146, 147, 149–50, 151

Seashore Construction Company: 98 (center right)

Dawn Shieferdecker (top): 34

Trinity Boys Choir, photo by Duo Dickinson: 47

United Technologies, photos by Spencer Sloan: 44

University of Connecticut Poinsettia Trials, photos by Richard McAvoy: 115, 116 (all except top left and bottom right, photos by Luma Abu Ayyash)

Valley Brook Community Church, photo by Bill Kole: 33 (bottom)

Jane Booth Vollers: iv, 2–3, 23 (all except center), 27 (all except bottom right), 34 (bottom), 67 (upper left, lower right), 71 (upper left, second row left), 87 (bottom left and right), 88, 91, 98 (center left), 117 (center right), 119 (second row left), 136, 141, 144 (center left), 145, 148, 154, 156

Wallingford Center, Inc.: 38 (bottom left)

Wesleyan Potters: 79 (top right)

Tom Woodruff: 4–6, 11, 21, 23 (center), 28, 30–32, 60 (bottom left and right), 61, 65–66, 74 (inset), 75 (bottom), 89 (bottom left, center right), 98 (bottom left and right), 101, 117 (bottom right), 128 (top left, center right), 132–33, 135, 144 (bottom left and right)

WTNH-TV: 155

Gail Zucker: 29, 33 (top), 67 (bottom center), 87 (center left), 120, 123, 127 (bottom left)

Acknowledgments

Christmas is a time for giving gifts, and the ones given to me that made this book possible are too numerous to catalog. This is a thank-you note for some of them.

To the team at Globe Pequot Press, thanks for your enthusiasm and your many talents. To Paula Brisco, the wonderful editor who wished for a white Christmas to set the scene for a beautiful book, be careful what you wish for! Thanks for your endless store of patience and encouragement. Nancy Freeborn, your designs make these pages a Christmas pageant. Jane Reilly, your boundless zest for this project helped carry me through a Christmas season that lingered into July. Thanks to Linda Kennedy, Mike Urban, Kevin Lynch, Saralyn D'Amato-Twomey, Dana Baylor, Melodie Goldstein Foster, Lisa Reneson, Angie Capone and, of course, Larry Dorfman.

To the team of photographers who fanned out across Connecticut to capture the spirit of the season, thank you! You found beauty and joy that others might have missed.

I am grateful to my friend and producer Michele Russo for hauling the brood around to get a kid's eye view of Christmas, for her endless devotion to this project and the TV special, and for her willingness to make "just one more call."

The companion Connecticut Public Broadcasting (CPTV) special would not have been possible without Arthur Diedrick, the President and Chairman of the Connecticut Development Authority, and John Klein, the President, Chairman and CEO of People's Bank. Thanks for believing.

Thank you to CPTV for embracing *Positively Connecticut,* and to Jerry Franklin and Larry Rifkin for making CPTV the place for telling the stories of Connecticut. Thanks to Bette Blackwell for bringing every story to life. Haig Papasian, thanks for always finding a way.

To my colleagues at WTIC NewsTalk 1080, thanks for understanding about deadlines.

To the people in these pages, and on screen who shared their stories, thanks for your Christmas spirit. You are positively Connecticut!

Christmas is all about family. Mom and Dad, thanks for making my memories of "Christmas past" magical. Thanks for staying up past midnight and getting up before dawn. To my brother and sisters and their families, thanks for filling our holidays with love and laughter. You make "home for the holidays" meaningful.

To my husband, Tom, thanks for making "Christmas present" beautiful. Your love and faith make all things possible.

Merry Christmas to all!

About the Author

Diane Smith is co-host of the Morning Show with Ray Dunaway on WTIC-AM NewsTalk 1080. She produces programs for Connecticut Public Television based on her popular series *Positively Connecticut™,* and she is the author of two books based on *Positively Connecticut* segments.

Diane was a news anchor and reporter at WTNH News Channel 8 in New Haven, Connecticut, for more than sixteen years, where her reporting earned her an Emmy Award. Her public affairs documentaries have earned state and national awards from the Associated Press, the Society of Professional Journalists, the National Commission against Drunk Driving, and other organizations.

She was awarded the Connecticut Tourism Industry's 1999 Media Award for *Positively Connecticut.* The American Cancer Society honored her for her work in educating women about breast cancer, and Domestic Violence Services of Greater New Haven gave Diane its Sofie Turner Award in March 2000 for her statewide work in promoting efforts to reduce domestic violence. Her extensive community service also includes work for Easter Seals, Leave a Legacy, IMPAC-CT State University Award for Young Writers, and The Women's Campaign School at Yale University.

Each year at Christmas, Diane is the voice of the United Illuminating Fantasy of Lights to benefit Easter Seals. She is currently the honorary chair of Lauralton Hall's Christmas in the Mansion, honorary chair of the Wadsworth Atheneum's Festival of Trees and Traditions, and honorary chair of the Junior League of Greater New Britain's Noel Boutique.

Born in Newark, New Jersey, and a graduate of the State University of New York at Binghamton, Diane lives on the Connecticut shoreline with her husband, Tom Woodruff, and her dogs Chancellor and Chester. She encourages readers to visit her Web site at www.positivelyct.com.

A holiday scene in Essex.